SHANNON RULLO

A HORROR LOVER'S COOKBOOK

T W I N S T A R
M E D I A

WWW.TWINSTARONLINE.COM

ABOUT THE AUTHOR

Shannon Rullo is the creator and writer of the horror and cooking column "Cannibal Kitchen." The column is currently being featured on the horror review website ZombiesDontRun.Net. In past years, she once spent the better part of a decade ghost-writing movies for Lucio Fulci. Some would say the famous "zombie versus shark" scene from the movie Zombie was really Shannon's idea; however, due to a massive and convenient fire, no documented proof exists to support these claims. When not cooking up gore, Shannon is a self-employed hairstylist at Roki Boki Art Salon and a volunteer at PAWS, Chicago's no-kill animal shelter.

I would like to thank…

My husband, Peter Rullo, for being just as quirky and ridiculous as I am. Also for being a willing participant in eating way to much over the past couple months and being able to give constructive criticism to someone who shares a bed with you. Thanks for always pushing me to challenge and better myself, with out you I don't believe the Cannibal Kitchen column would exist.

Chuck Conry, for being my Internet partner in crime. We set out years ago for world domination and I don't think we're doing to shabby. Thank you for always being a stand up guy, being there when many others weren't, and being the best friend I could ask for even if we've never met in real life.

Anyone who has ever read or supported my column, Cannibal Kitchen. Without any of you guys, this wouldn't have been possible. I appreciate it. I appreciate all your comments and suggestions.

My family, who has helped create the person that I am today. I have a drive, stubbornness, and a "never give up" attitude because of you guys.

My in-laws, for continuous support in this project, and embracing me with open arms.

The amazing ladies I work with at Roki Boki Art Salon. Over the years you guys have become more like family to me than co-workers. I wouldn't trade our conversations or knowing you all for anything in the world.

Joe Montalto of Doom&Gloom Photography, for doing an amazing job on the pictures for this cookbook and in general being one of the best photographers I've ever had the pleasure to work with.

John Aranza of Horrorbles, for being one of the coolest people I've ever met! Thank you for lending out your store with open arms to a fellow horror fiend to do a photo shoot in. Everyone should take note and shop local. Support Independent businesses.

Chris Gutierrez, for fielding numerous questions from me over the past couple of months and never making me feel like I was bothering you. You've been a huge help and I appreciate it.

Joe Shanahan and all of Metro staff for always being extremely generous and hospitable over the years.

Doug Sohn, of "Hot Doug's", for making Mondays better and always being big hearted with your help.

Any and all of my friends whom have let me cook for them, listened to me babble over the past couple months about recipes, and have stood with me through the years no matter the ups and down or the situation. You all have made me a better person and for that I am grateful.

Tony Schaab at TwinStar Media, for taking a leap of faith on a girl you only knew through an online column. TwinStar has been wonderful to work with and more than I can express, I am grateful for this opportunity.

Cover design: Tom Schriner
Cover picture: Joe Montalto of Doom&Gloom Photography
Food pictures: Shannon Rullo
Interior design and layout: Tom Schriner and Tony Schaab

TABLE OF CONTENTS

ZOMBIE-PLAGUED PIZZAS

MANIACAL MAIN COURSES

B-RATED DESSERTS

A HORROR LOVER'S COOKBOOK

On a brisk February night an indeterminate number of years ago, I came out of my mother's womb with a *Night of the Living Dead* VHS in one hand and a machete in the other. Since that day, I have embraced my destiny and not looked back. Nurtured by the mean streets of Chicago, I quickly became one with the idea that hot dogs don't need ketchup, and I embraced the fact that "Cubs Fan" was a dirty word in my household.

Growing up in an Italian and Greek family taught me a few important things: that food was very important, that I was cursed to talk with my hands, and that (according to my Papa) everyone should own a donkey. Unfortunately, I still haven't gotten my donkey, but on a happier note, my Grandma did teach everyone that *Killer Klowns from Outer Space* was the only thing that could keep me entertained and quiet as a child. I think that was what the idea of "babysitting" was in the 1980s. Man, the '80s were great.

As of today, I pay rent on the north side of Chicago and share my space with two black cats named Zoey and Varg that destroy my houseplants. There is also a guy named Peter who likes to hang around and eat the food I cook. He says he is my husband, but I don't know if I believe him. He seems to have pictures as proof, along with some legal documents, so I'm guessing he's onto something.

When I am not making people pretty, I spend most of my down time pairing two things I love dearly: horror and food. I created the Cannibal Kitchen column some time in 2010, and luckily for me, I was offered a gracious home at ZombiesDontRun.Net. Chuck Conry (creator of ZDR) and I had been planning world domination for years leading up to this, so it was really the only logical option. Since my first post, Cannibal Kitchen has grown by leaps and bounds; every movie review and recipe gets a little piece of my soul, and I thoroughly have enjoyed watching my baby grow.

I am happy to be able to share my first cookbook with you all. It's important for me to bring you kitschy recipes that won't make your head or wallet hurt. You will see a lot of classic dishes with a new twist, and a ton of user-friendly ingredients that won't make you go running for the dictionary. However, I can't guarantee that, depending on which movie you are watching while eating said recipes, you won't go running with projectile vomit to the garbage can. Is it in bad taste to talk about vomiting in a cookbook?

Shannon Rullo

P.S. Fire extinguisher not included.

" The seven dreaded gateways to Hell are concealed in seven cursed places…and from the day the gates of Hell are opened, the dead will walk the earth."

beyond your basic bruschetta

the beyond

Whom do I have to kill to inherit a hotel that lays over one of the gates to Hell? I mean come on, I like to explore odd places, and I enjoy unseasonably warm weather. *The Beyond* is, in my opinion, one of the more underrated films by one of Italy's finest filmmakers, Lucio Fulci. Fulci was a movie-making magician, and he became a true master at perfecting gore as an art form. From start to finish, *The Beyond* never disappoints in the stomach-churning department. Much like Fulci, I also never like to disappoint in the stomach-churning department. That's why I took this basic bruschetta and spruced it up with some tangy goat cheese. I guarantee you this is finger food Fulci wouldn't have minded taking back to the old country. Mangia!

directions:

Preheat oven to 350 Degrees. Mix together all bruschetta ingredients except the bread, and chill covered for 1 hour. In a food processor, mix together all the goat cheese ingredients, and set aside. Next, on a baking sheet lie out the cut bread and lightly brush the tops with olive oil. Bake for 5 minutes to gently toast.

To assemble the bruschetta, spread a generous amount of goat cheese on the toasted bread, followed by a generous spoonful of the tomato mixture. Follow with a little sprinkle of chopped basil over the tops.

Makes 8

ingredients:

Beyond your Basic Bruschetta ingredients:
1 Loaf French Bread, Cut into 1 inch slices
3 Medium Vine Ripe Tomatoes, diced
1/3 Cup Red Onion, diced
¼ Cup Olive Oil
1 Tablespoon Balsamic Vinegar
¼ Cup fresh Basil, Diced, more to garnish
¼ Teaspoon Salt
¼ Teaspoon Black Pepper

Liza's Gory Goat Cheese Spread ingredients:
1 (4 ounce) Package Goat Cheese
2 Tablespoons Pesto
1 Tablespoon Garlic
¼ Teaspoon Salt
¼ Teaspoon Pepper

"Nothing has ever stripped your nerves as screamingly raw as the Gore Gore Girls."

the gore gore guac

the gore gore girls

Wait, a movie about strippers dying in a Chicago nightclub? Are you sure this isn't a documentary? I try to work this movie into most conversations I have based on the fact that I just enjoy saying the title of the movie. Come on now; say it with me: *The Gore Gore Girls*. It just rolls of the tongue so nicely. Besides a great title, this movie is a great combination of intentional and unintentional humor and extreme gore shots. Herschell Gordon Lewis has a very distinct style to his films, and *The Gore Gore Girls* is no different. However, being that Lewis had originally intended this to be his last film (and it was, until he un-retired 30 years later to direct 2002's *Blood Feast 2*), I do believe he really made a point to go above and beyond in the gore department. Anyone care for a French fried face? No? Well, then how about some Gore Gore Guac, a semi-spicy and creamy take on your every day guacamole.

ingredients:

3 Avocados, halved, peeled, and pitted
Juice from ½ a Lime
¼ Cup Sour Cream
¼ Cup Red Onion, diced
1/3 Cup Fresh Cilantro, chopped
1 Tablespoon Jalapeños, seeded and diced
¼ Cup Tomato, diced
1 Tablespoon Cream Cheese
½ Teaspoon Salt
½ Teaspoon Garlic Powder
¼ Teaspoon Black Pepper

directions:

In a medium sized bowl, take a fork and mash the avocado with the lime juice, cream cheese, and sour cream. Mix the salt, garlic powder, and black pepper into the avocado mix. In a small bowl, mix together all other ingredients, and then transfer them to the avocado mixture. Stir to completely combine and serve.

Serves 4-6

macready's corndog muffins

the thing

The Thing is a movie pretty much everyone knows. Hopefully, in this case, it's for having seen the 1982 version and not the sad excuse for a prequel that was released in 2011. I've heard people be as harsh as saying that they can't wait for John Carpenter to die so he can roll over in his grave about that one. Ouch! R.J. MacReady was a man of all men. How could you not be, with a beard like that, and the wit and charm to back it up? Lucky for us, there were no female characters in this movie; nothing would have gotten done around camp, because it would have been a panty-dropping fest. Although I haven't dropped any panties with these corndog muffins, maybe you can have better luck in that department. Who wouldn't want a mini-corn bread muffin filled with a meaty hot dog?

directions:

Preheat oven to 400 Degrees. Cut each hot dog into about 1 inch pieces, and set aside. In a large bowl, mix together the flour, cornmeal, eggs, sugar, salt, cayenne pepper, and baking powder. Next, add all remaining ingredients except hot dogs. In a lightly greased mini-cupcake tin, fill each circle 50 percent full with corn bread batter. Gently set one piece of the cut hotdog into the center, and lightly push it down with your index finger until it is almost to the bottom. Spoon enough batter over the top to completely cover the hotdog. Bake for 15-20 minutes.

Makes 24

ingredients:

1 Cup All-purpose Flour
1 Cup Yellow Cornmeal
1 Cup Buttermilk
½ Cup Butter
½ Cup Pepper Jack Cheese, grated
2/3 Cup Sugar
¼ Cup Sour cream
2 Eggs
1 Teaspoon Baking Powder
½ Teaspoon Salt
½ Teaspoon Cayenne Pepper
1 Package Hot Dogs
1 Mini Cupcake Tin

pinhead pinwheels

hellraiser

Is it just me, or can anyone else not shake the fact Pinhead must walk around with one hell of a headache on a regular basis? It's kind of a shame what has happened to the *Hellraiser* franchise. Pinhead started out as such a great character in a storyline that took a different route in a decade that rained slasher films. Unfortunately, what has become of the series is kind of a turd-fest at this point. I will now only refer to these recent releases as the "dark days." These Pinhead Pinwheels feature the great ham-like taste of prosciutto, and accentuate it perfectly with the bold taste of mozzarella and melon. Even better, they come in bite sized fancy sandwiches and fight off the Cenobites.

ingredients:

3 Large Soft Tortilla Shells
15 slices Prosciutto
18 slices Fresh Mozzarella
3 Big Lettuce Leaves
1 (8oz) Cream Cheese, softened
1 Tablespoon Mustard
¼ Cup Honeydew Melon, diced
¼ Tablespoon Oregano
Saran Wrap
Toothpicks

directions:

In a medium sized bowl, mix together the cream cheese, mustard, melon, and oregano. On each tortilla shell, spread a generous amount of the cream cheese mixture, leaving about 1 inch around the perimeter of the circle untouched. Follow this by putting 1 piece of lettuce, 6 slices of mozzarella, and 5 slices of prosciutto on each tortilla, leaving about 1-½ inches around the perimeter of the circle untouched.

Next, roll each tortilla into a cylinder shape as tightly as you can. Take a piece of saran wrap and wrap it tightly around the cylinder roll of tortilla. Secure with about 4 toothpicks evenly spread out and inserted through the saran wrap. Refrigerate for 3 hours to help stabilize the shape of the pinwheel.

After 3 hours, remove and take off the saran wrap and toothpicks. With a sharp knife, cut each cylinder into ½ inch slices.

Makes about 15

Suspiria

un film de **DARIO ARGENTO**

"Once you've seen it, you will never again feel safe in the dark."

suspiria sliders

suspiria

Suspiria is one of my favorite movies, and growing up, White Castle sliders became somewhat of a delicacy in my house. I already know what you're thinking, and I don't see anything wrong with either of those statements. *Suspiria* showcases an American girl in a German ballet school; now throw in a little cult-like action, a few witches, and some dying students, and you have what many people like to refer to as Dario Argento's masterpiece. Besides an all around great story line and good kills, the one thing that sold me on this film was the beautiful use of color with the cinematography. Argento accomplished such a rich color palette in a way uncommon for that time period. The film was shot on a normal Eastman Color Kodak stock, and then printed using the 3-strip Technicolor process, utilizing one of the last remaining machines. I'm impressed, and I'm sure all your party guests will be equally as impressed when you pop in this movie and then surprise them with this grown-up version of the White Castle slider.

ingredients:

Suspiria Sliders ingredients:
1 ½ Pounds Ground Chuck
½ Cup White Onion, diced
1 Egg
1 Tablespoon Minced garlic
½ Teaspoon Salt
½ Teaspoon Black Pepper
8 Hawaiian Rolls

Pillage and Burn Pickled Cucumber ingredients:
1 Cucumber, sliced thin
1 ½ Cups White Vinegar
½ Cup Water
2 Garlic cloves, Crushed and diced
1 Teaspoon Balsamic Vinegar
1 Teaspoon Salt
1 Teaspoon Sugar
½ Teaspoon Black Pepper

Zesty Suzy Sauce ingredients:
½ Cup Mayonnaise
2 Tablespoons Ketchup
2 Teaspoons Yellow Mustard
1 ½ Teaspoons Horseradish sauce
½ Teaspoon Sugar
½ Teaspoon Lemon Juice
½ Teaspoon Cumin
½ Teaspoon Cayenne Pepper
½ Teaspoon Black Pepper
¼ Teaspoon Salt

directions:

First, make the pickled cucumbers the day before by combining the white vinegar, water, and balsamic. Follow by adding the spices and mixing to combine. With the chopped cucumbers in a medium sized bowl, add the vinegar mixture and toss to evenly coat. Cover and refrigerate for 24 hours. The following day, prepare the Zesty Suzy sauce by mixing all sauce ingredients together and refrigerating, covered, for at least 1 hour. To make the Suspiria Slider patties, mix all ingredients together in a large bowl. Next, form the meat mixture into 8 tightly packed small patties. In a large, lightly greased pan, cook the patties for 4-5 minutes per side, over a medium-to-high heat, or until desired doneness.

Assemble the sliders by placing 1 patty on each Hawaiian roll, followed by some zesty sauce, a couple pickled cucumbers, and the top bun. Add cheese if your heart desires, but they're perfect without.

Makes 8

*"Beware the ball,
beware the tall man,
beware the never dead."*

the tall man's tiny pretzel bites

phantasm

Don Coscarelli went above and beyond with the movie *Phantasm* and the character that is eerily known only as "Tall Man." On this film, Coscarelli was somewhat a "jack of all trades" or, depending on how you look at it, a complete control freak: not only did he write and produce the film, he also directed, was the DP, the editor, and I wouldn't be shocked to find out that he made coffee and did all the hair and makeup on set as well. Can anyone say micro managing? Regardless, I have zero complaints about this movie. It's perfectly quirky and bizarre, has strange Jawa-looking creatures, and a terrifying main character. These Tall Man Tiny Pretzel Bites have the perfect amount of spice, and pair perfectly with this homemade beer cheese dip. One bite and you'll want to micro-manage this platter, Coscarelli style.

ingredients:

The Tall Man's Tiny Pretzel Bites ingredients:
1 (1/4 Ounce) Package Dry Active Yeast
1 ½ Cups Warm Water
3 Tablespoons Butter, melted and reserved for later
1 Tablespoon Butter, melted
1 Tablespoon Sugar
1 Tablespoon Light Brown Sugar
4 Cups and 3 Tablespoons All-purpose Flour
1 Teaspoon Salt
1 Teaspoon Garlic Powder
1/3 Cup Jalapeños, seeded and chopped
Coarse Sea Salt to garnish
Parchment Paper

Coscarelli Cheese Dip ingredients:
½ Can Cheddar Cheese Soup
2 Cups Sharp Cheddar, shredded
¼ Cup Cream Cheese, softened
¾ Cup Beer
2 Tablespoons Spicy Mustard
2 Tablespoons Chives, diced

directions:

Preheat the oven to 425 Degrees. In a large bowl, combine the water, both sugars, yeast, and 1 Tablespoon of butter. Let stand for 5 minutes or until the mixture becomes bubbly (if it doesn't bubble, your yeast is bad). In a medium-sized bowl, sift together the flour, salt, and garlic. Gradually add the flour mixture to the yeast mixture and mix until the dough is smooth and pliable, usually about 4 minutes. Next, add in the diced jalapenos, and mix just enough to combine. If the dough appears too wet, add additional flour in 1 tablespoon increments.

In a small bowl, melt 2 tablespoons of butter, and line a baking sheet with parchment paper. Next, divide the dough into 4 portions to make it easier to handle. Roll each portion into ropes that are about 1 Inch in diameter, and then cut into 1 inch pieces. Roll each piece of dough in the melted butter, and then place on the lined baking sheet. Sprinkle with coarse sea salt and bake for 8-10 minutes, or until golden brown.

To make the Coscarelli Cheese Dip, in a medium saucepan bring half a can of Cheddar Cheese Soup mixed with the beer to a boil. On low heat, gradually add both cheeses and mustard, and then cook for another 5 minutes, stirring constantly. Remove and garnish with diced chives.

Serves 4-6

"Now get out of my way, Henry, or I swear to god you'll be wearing your balls for earrings!"

wilma's severed wings

creepshow

Wilma Northrup was, what we like to call in the Windy City, a B-I-T-C-H. A character in one of *Creepshow's* five jolting tales of horror, Wilma does everything she can to make her husband Henry's life difficult. I'm sure in real life we have all met a "Wilma" a time or two. The key difference in the film is that Henry has the ability to do what we've all secretly wanted to do to these types of people for ages: feed said person to a beast that lives in a crate. I know I'm jealous. This delightful finger food has a great smoked and sweet meaty taste, probably unlike the taste featured by that shrew of a woman Wilma and her type.

ingredients:

Monster Marinade ingredients:
3 Tablespoons Butter, melted
2 Tablespoons Honey
1 Egg, beaten
Smoked Mesquite Seasoning, Black Pepper, and Salt to taste

Sideshow Surprise ingredients:
1 Package Boneless Chicken Breast Tenderloins
1 Package Maple Bacon, thin cut
1 Bottle of your preferred BBQ Sauce
(I use Sweet Baby Rays)
Light Brown Sugar
Toothpicks

directions:

In a small bowl, melt the butter, and then add the honey and beaten egg. Mix to fully combine. Place the chicken in a small pan and pour the butter-honey combo over it. Sprinkle liberally with all three spices. Cover and refrigerate for 1 hour. While sitting, the liquid mixture may take a semi-hardened form; this is normal.

Next, preheat the oven to 350 Degrees; in a large glass baking dish, bake the chicken for 10 minutes. Remove from oven, and then assemble by basting with BBQ sauce and then wrapping one piece of bacon around each tenderloin. If you are having a hard time getting the bacon to stay, just secure with a toothpick. Sprinkle each piece with a little brown sugar and then return the food to the oven for 15 minutes. After the time is up, remove from the oven and baste liberally with more BBQ sauce, sprinkle with more brown sugar, and return the food to the oven for a final 15 minutes.

Makes 6-8

"Can they be stopped?"

ash's fried asparagus

the evil dead

If you haven't yet seen *The Evil Dead*, I order you to put down this book right this instant and helicopter yourself in a copy. You'll laugh, you'll cry, but most of all, you will fall in love with Bruce Campbell's character, Ashley "Ash" Williams. There are brainless teenagers, possession, evil, and a disturbing forest scene that will make you think twice before becoming a tree-hugger. Since I don't like to eat trees, I figured a good way to avenge Cheryl's "mishap" would be to eat a stalk of asparagus. Oh, and not just any asparagus, but a stalk of asparagus fried and soaking in my spicy red pepper mustard sauce.

ingredients:

Ash's Fried Asparagus ingredients:
1 Pound Asparagus, trimmed
1 ½ Cups All-Purpose Flour
1 Cup Fine Cornmeal
1 Cup Buttermilk
½ Cup Beer
1 Egg
½ Teaspoon Cumin
½ Teaspoon Salt
½ Teaspoon Oregano
1 Teaspoon Onion Powder
Vegetable or Peanut Oil for frying

Cheryl's Vengeance Sauce ingredients:
4 Tablespoons Dijon Mustard
2 Tablespoons Honey
1 Tablespoon Sriracha Hot Chili Sauce
½ Teaspoon Minced Garlic
2 Tablespoons Red Pepper, finely diced
3 Tablespoons Olive Oil

directions:

In a small bowl, mix together all of the Cheryl's Vengeance Sauce ingredients, and then pour into a small saucepan. Over low heat, sauté the mixture for 5 minutes. Pour the mixture back in the bowl, and allow the flavors to blend together while you fry the asparagus.

To make the fried asparagus, heat 1 ½ inches of oil in a frying pan or deep fryer set to 335 Degrees. Next, take a large zip-lock bag and fill it with ½ cup of flour. Put the trimmed asparagus into the bag and shake to coat. In a small bowl, mix together the beer, buttermilk, and egg. In a large bowl, mix together the seasonings and 1 cup flour. Add the beer mixture to flour mixture and stir to combine. Dip asparagus into batter and then fry for 5 minutes or until golden brown. Drain on paper towel and then serve with the spicy mustard sauce drizzled over the top.

Makes about 20

"What's the matter, kid?
Don't ya like clowns?"

captain spaulding's spuds

house of 1,000 corpses
the devil's rejects

Captain Spaulding is a genius character. Whether you are watching *House of 1000 Corpses* or *The Devil's Rejects*, the stuff that comes out of Sid Haig's mouth is gut-spewing gold. It's no secret that I'm not a huge fan of clowns, however this is one clown I wouldn't mind whipping together these seasoned tater tots for. They are overflowing with flavor and crispiness as is, or you can dip them in a little ketchup; it's up to you to pick your poison.

ingredients:

2 Large sized Baking Potatoes, peeled and finely shredded
6 Tablespoons All-Purpose Flour
1 Tablespoon Seasoning Salt
1 Teaspoon Garlic Salt
1 Teaspoon Onion Salt
1 Teaspoon Basil
1 Teaspoon Minced Onion
½ Teaspoon Cayenne Pepper
¼ Teaspoon Salt
1 Egg, beaten
Vegetable Oil for frying

directions:

Heat ¼ inch of oil in a frying pan or set a deep fryer to 335 Degrees. Place the potatoes in a food processor and finely shred. It's important to take the shredded potatoes and then put them in a colander to push out all excess water.

Pour potatoes into a medium-sized bowl and add the remainder of the ingredients, with the flour being last. Next, form the potato mixture into tot-like balls about the size of 1 Teaspoon, drop them into the oil, and fry until slightly golden; about 8-10 minutes. If the tots are getting too dark too fast, that means your oil is too hot and it needs to be turned down. Remove and drain on a paper towel. Have extras? No problem, because these freeze and re-heat beautifully.

Serves 2

WILLIAM PETER BLATTY'S

THE EXORCIST

Directed by WILLIAM FRIEDKIN

Something almost beyond comprehension is happening to a girl on this street, in this house ...and a man has been sent for as a last resort. The man is The Exorcist.

ELLEN BURSTYN · MAX VON SYDOW · LEE J. COBB
JACK MacGOWRAN · JASON MILLER
WILLIAM PETER BLATTY

"Somewhere between science and superstition, there is another world. The world of darkness."

the exorsalad

the exorcist

The Exorcist is with out a doubt a cult classic. I'd be lying if I said I hadn't thought about turning my sunroom into a shrine room a time or two. Hitting the big screen in 1973, this movie was far ahead of its time. It featured a foul-mouth child doing stuff with a cross that made even me blush. It must have made others blush too, because one viewer even fainted in a theater, resulting in a broken jaw and a lawsuit. Some say all Regan needed was an exorcist; I personally think she just needed a little of my Caprese-inspired salad. The power of Italian flavoring compels you!

directions:

Dice up the tomatoes and mozzarella, and put them in a medium-sized bowl. Add the chopped-up basil and mix to combine. In a small bowl, mix all the other ingredients. Pour the liquid mixture over the tomato mixture, and mix to evenly coat. If needed, add additional salt and pepper to your liking.

Serves 3-4

ingredients:

1 (Dry Pint) Package Grape Tomatoes Cut in halves
1 (12 ounce) Package Mini Mozzarella balls marinated in oil and red pepper flakes, halved
6 Basil leaves, chopped
1 Teaspoon Minced Garlic
3 Tablespoons Olive Oil
2 Tablespoons Balsamic Vinegar
1 Teaspoon Salt
1 Teaspoon Black Pepper
½ Teaspoon Dijon Mustard

"After it was all over…she waited…then she struck back in a way only a woman can!"

i spit on your pasta salad

i spit on your grave

In my opinion, *I Spit On Your Grave* shouldn't be a movie, but more of a guideline to life. If you act like a complete scumbag, then I think you willingly open yourself up to having some spiteful woman wreak revenge on your genitals with a knife. Originally referred to as *Day of the Woman*, Roger Ebert once dubbed this as the "worst movie ever made." Yes, I get that the content of the movie makes *Deliverance* look like a Disney movie; however, I believe that it's a great portrayal of the fact that not every woman is going to sit around and just play the victim. I own a very rare cut of this film; in my version, after Jennifer kills everyone, she strolls into the woods with a bowl of my Italian-style pasta salad. What you didn't get this extended-cut version?

ingredients:

I Spit On Your Pasta Salad ingredients:
1 (8 oz) Box Bow Tie Pasta
½ Cup Plum Tomatoes, halved
1 (2 oz) Can Black Olives
3 Stalks Celery, chopped
½ White Onion, diced
1 Cup Cheddar Cheese, diced into cubes
1 Cup Pepperoni, diced into cubes

Day of the Dressing ingredients:
1 Cup Olive Oil
½ Cup White wine vinegar
2 Tablespoons Balsamic Vinegar
1 Teaspoon Dried Oregano
1 Tablespoon Water
1 Tablespoon Onion Powder
1 Teaspoon Garlic Powder
1 Tablespoon Minced Garlic
1 Teaspoon Sugar
1 Teaspoon Salt
½ Teaspoon Black Pepper
1 Teaspoon Red Pepper Flakes
1 Teaspoon Dried Basil
½ Teaspoon Lemon Juice
¼ Teaspoon Dried Thyme

directions:

Although not necessary, I recommend making the salad dressing the day before and allowing the mixture to sit covered in the refrigerator for 24 hours. This allows all the spices to settle, and it creates the perfect amount of love necessary for flavor overload. To make the dressing: in a small Tupperware-like container, mix all the ingredients and 4 Tablespoons of the spice mixture together and chill. Upon sitting, settling of the spices is normal. The next day, just give the container a good shake, and it's ready to party.

In a medium-sized saucepan, cook the pasta according to manufacturer's directions. Drain and place in a large mixing bowl. Add all the remaining ingredients to the bowl of pasta, and then pour all the dressing in as well. Toss the mixture to completely coat everything, and then cover and chill for 1 hour before serving. Upon removing from the refrigerator, taste the pasta salad and add more salt and pepper to your liking.

Serves 6

MORJANA ALAOUI · MYLÈNE JAMPANOI

MARTYRS

UN FILM DE

"Martyrs are exceptional people. They survive pain, they survive total deprivation. They bear all the sins of the earth."

mademoiselle's martyberry salad

martyrs

Keeping with the French theme, *Martyrs* is a French film that delivers on every level. There is gore, a crazy shotgun scene, suffering in the name of religion, and a full body skinning. So if you ever want to be the "coolest kid" in the room, just pop this movie on, make this strawberry-flavored summer salad, and then watch everyone scatter within 15 minutes.

ingredients:

1 (5 oz) Bag of Baby Spinach
20 Strawberries, chopped
½ Cup Red Onion, chopped
½ Cup Cucumber, chopped
½ Cup Feta Crumbles
½ Cup Olive Oil
1 Tablespoon Balsamic Vinegar
1 Tablespoon Superfine Sugar
1 Teaspoon Dijon Mustard
½ Teaspoon Salt

directions:

In a large bowl, put the spinach, 6 chopped strawberries, onion, cucumber, and feta; then set aside. In a medium saucepan, put the remaining strawberries, 2 Tablespoons of water, and the sugar; cook on low heat for 5 minutes. Remove the fruit and place a sieve over a medium-sized bowl; press firmly with a spoon to fully drain. Allow the strawberry liquid to cool, and then add the remainder of the ingredients and stir until the mustard dissolves. Pour the liquid into the bowl of spinach, and toss to cover evenly.

Serves 3-4

EIN FILM ÜBER DIE LIEBE ZUM MENSCHEN
UND WAS VON IHM ÜBRIG BLEIBT

NEKRomantik

MANFRED JELINSKI präsentiert »NEKROMANTIK«   Ein Film von JÖRG BUTTGEREIT

Mit DAKTARI LORENZ · BEATRICE M. · HARALD LUNDT · SUSA KOHLSTEDT · HEIKE S.

Kamera UWE BOHRER   Musik J. B. WALTON · H. KOPP · D. LORENZ

Buch JÖRG BUTTGEREIT · FRANZ RODENKIRCHEN   Produktion MANFRED O. JELINSKI

Regie JÖRG BUTTGEREIT

"Death is just the beginning."

nekromixed veggies

nekromantik

I still stand firm that *Nekromantik* is one of the most screwed-up movies I have ever seen. This low-budget gore-shocker features an odd man by the name of Rob. Rob thinks it's a great idea to bring home a corpse one day, only to find that his wife Betty doesn't seem to mind if her sexual partners aren't so, ahem, fresh…if you get my drift.

If you are now slightly disgusted and tend to care what you put in your mouth, then this mixed veggie salad is right up your alley. Fresh as can be and cooked in a maple Dijon, fall-inspired dressing, this salad is guaranteed to taste a bit better than rotting flesh.

ingredients:

2 Pounds Yukon Gold Potatoes, halved
2 Zucchinis, chopped into cubes
2 Carrots, chopped
1 Yellow Onion, chopped
1 Cup Maple Syrup
2 Tablespoons Jack Daniels
2 Tablespoons Dijon Mustard
2 Tablespoons Olive Oil
1 Tablespoon Minced Garlic
1 Tablespoon Butter, melted
1 Teaspoon Honey
1 Teaspoon Chili Sauce
1 Teaspoon Sugar
1 Teaspoon Black Pepper
1 Teaspoon Pumpkin Pie Seasoning
¼ Teaspoon Black Pepper
¼ Teaspoon Salt

directions:

Preheat oven to 400 Degrees. Place the vegetables in a 9 x 13 inch casserole dish. In a medium-sized mixing bowl, stir together all the other ingredients until they are completely combined. Next, pour the mixture over all the vegetables and mix until everything is evenly coated. Cover with foil and bake for 25 minutes. After 25 minutes, remove from the oven; with a spoon, mix all the ingredients together again, making sure the vegetables remain coated. Return to the oven, turn down the temperature to 350 Degrees, and continue to bake for another 25 minutes covered. After, remove from the oven once more, toss again, and return the oven for an additional 15 minutes uncovered. Serve as is, or with a little of the remaining sauce poured over them.

Serves 6-8

YOU HAVE BEEN WARNED

IF SOMETHING
FRIGHTENING
HAPPENS TO YOU
TODAY,
THINK ABOUT IT

IT MAY BE

THE OMEN

GREGORY PECK   LEE REMICK
THE OMEN
A HARVEY BERNHARD-MACE NEUFELD PRODUCTION
DAVID WARNER   BILLIE WHITELAW
MACE NEUFELD   HARVEY BERNHARD   RICHARD DONNER
DAVID SELTZER

"Those who foretold it are dead. Those who can stop it are in grave danger."

the omac

the omen

The Omen cursed the big screen at a time the horror genre was turning. Unlike some of his gore-filled competition, Director Richard Donner dabbled his hands in something a little bit more eerie and tested peoples beliefs in religion. Dabbled he did, and success he had. *The Omen* has easily become a cult classic and made Damien a household name. Lucky for me, in my house, the Devil took a back seat and this Mac and Cheese became a household name. Rich and velvety in texture, this is a side dish that your soul won't mind getting the evil eye from.

ingredients:

1 (8 oz) package of Macaroni
4 Tablespoons Butter, softened
3 Tablespoons All-Purpose Flour
4 Cups Chicken Stock
2 1/3 Cups Whole Milk
1 Cup Sharp Cheddar, preferably aged and of good quality, grated
1 Cup Colby Jack, preferably aged and of good quality, grated
1 ½ Teaspoons Fresh Chives, chopped
1 Teaspoon Salt
1 Teaspoon Black Pepper
1 Teaspoon Minced Onion
1 Teaspoon Minced Garlic
Seasoned Bread Crumbs

directions:

Preheat the oven to 350 Degrees. In a large pot, bring the chicken stock to a boil. Add the macaroni, cook according to manufacturer's directions, and set aside. In another large saucepan over medium heat, melt the butter and then add the flour; stir to combine. Next, add the milk and all seasonings. Reduce heat to low, and stir constantly for about 5 minutes. The flour needs to become completely dissolved.

After 5 minutes, turn the heat up to high and bring the mixture to a boil; allow to boil for 2 minutes, while stirring constantly. Reduce heat to low and cook for 10 minutes, still stirring constantly. Next, add both grated cheeses little by little, and mix until completely melted (about 3 minutes). Take the cooked macaroni, add it to the saucepan, and mix to combine. Make sure to taste the mixture and add a little more salt and pepper to your liking. Next, transfer the macaroni and cheese to an 8 x 11 baking dish. Sprinkle a small amount of the breadcrumbs over the top. Cover with foil and bake for 15 minutes.

Serves 4

"Pray it doesn't happen to you."

rabid ranch salad

rabid

If I could, I would hug David Cronenberg for making the movie *Rabid*. Some people like to argue that Cronenberg didn't get his act together until the '80s with movies such as *Videodrome* and *Deadzone*. I like to argue that these people are wrong. In 1977, we get *Rabid*, a film from Cronenberg that comes off as one part Vampire and one part Zombie. Even better, it features an at-times topless Marilyn Chambers. Boom chicka bow wow! While watching *Rabid*, some people seem to think that the characters are foaming at the mouth due to rabies; I like to think it's just because they are dying to get a bite of my spicy and sweet ranch dressing salad. You get a rich and creamy heat from the dressing itself, only to be spin-kicked by the sweet maple flavor of the pecans. It's a black eye you won't mind getting over and over again.

directions:

In a medium-sized bowl, mix together all the dressing ingredients, then chill covered for 1 hour. After the hour, mix all salad ingredients in a large bowl and set aside. In a medium-sized bowl, mix together the crushed almonds and maple syrup. Transfer the almond mixture to a medium skillet over low heat, and then pour the powdered sugar over the top. Begin mixing the sugar and almonds until the sugar starts to brown and the consistency gets gooey (about 5 minutes). Pour the ranch dressing in the salad bowl and toss to coat. Garnish with caramelized almonds.

Serves 4

ingredients:

Rabid Ranch Salad ingredients:
3 Heads Romaine, Washed and chopped
1/3 Cup Green Olives
¼ Cup Cranberries

Rabid Ranch Dressing ingredients:
½ Cup Sour Cream
½ Cup Mayonnaise
¼ Cup Buttermilk
1 Tablespoon Apple Cider Vinegar
1 Tablespoon Minced Garlic
2 Tablespoons Mild Green chilies, diced
¼ Teaspoon Black Pepper
¼ Teaspoon Cayenne Pepper
¼ Teaspoon Oregano
¼ Teaspoon Salt
¼ Teaspoon Marjoram

Marilyn Chambers' Caramelized Almonds ingredients:
½ Cup Almonds, Crushed
2 Tablespoons Maple Syrup
¼ Cup Powdered Sugar

"Pray for Rosemary's Baby."

rosemary's baby carrots

rosemary's baby

I think there should be one day a year dubbed "Rosemary's Baby Day." On said day, everyone will have to wear Mia Farrow wigs and chant in tongues. Some people deem this movie to be perfect; I believe perfect is in the eye of the beholder, however this film is probably about as close as you're going to get to universal perfection. The attention to detail director Roman Polanski paid to this movie is top notch. On the other hand, the attention your guests will pay to these honey and brown butter-roasted baby carrots will make breeding with Satan seem like a child's game.

ingredients:

2 Cups Baby Carrots
¼ Cup Honey
3 Tablespoons Butter, melted
1 Tablespoon Olive Oil
1 Teaspoon Light Brown sugar
½ Teaspoon Garlic Powder
¼ Teaspoon Salt
¼ Teaspoon Black Pepper
Foil

directions:

Preheat oven to 350 Degrees. In a small bowl melt the butter, and then add all the remaining ingredients except the carrots to the butter. Mix until everything is thoroughly combined and the honey has dissolved. Put the carrots in a medium-sized bowl and then add the butter mixture. Stir until the carrots are completely coated. Rip two pieces of foil into strips 1ft long. Place the carrot mixture into the center of the foil, and then fold the foil to form a tightly-closed pocket. Repeat this step again with the remaining carrots, forming another foil pouch. Bake for 1 hour.

Serves 2

"Christmas Eve..."

sheitan spiced beans

sheitan

I've said it before and I'll say it again, foreign horror movies are usually some of the best ever made. I don't know how they do it, but the French always seem to outdo themselves when it comes to the gore, substance, and all around twistedness of a film. *Sheitan* is no exception; people either seem to love or hate this film, and it is usually compared to a more perverse and satanic version of *The Texas Chainsaw Massacre*. I say you can't go wrong with a French film, or a dish of baked beans mixed in a bacon-flavored barbeque sauce. Don't agree? I'm sure Joseph, the evil and twisted star of the film, will give you an ending you won't soon forget.

ingredients:

5 Slices of Bacon
½ Cup Apple Cider Vinegar
1 ½ Cups White Onion, diced
2 Garlic Cloves, Crushed and diced
1 Cup Ketchup
2 Teaspoons Worcestershire Sauce
½ Cup Honey
2 Tablespoons Soy Sauce
2 Tablespoons Light Brown sugar
1 Teaspoon Jack Daniels Whiskey
½ Teaspoon Black Pepper
1 Teaspoon Hot Chili Sauce
½ Teaspoon Cinnamon
2 (15 oz) cans of Red Kidney Beans

directions:

Preheat oven to 300 Degrees. Cook the bacon and onions in a medium skillet over medium heat until crispy. Once cooked, remove the bacon and crumble into small pieces. Next, pour 1 Tablespoon of the cooked bacon grease and onions into a small saucepan. Sauté the mixture together over medium heat for 1 minute. Follow by adding all the remaining ingredients except the beans. Continue to whisk almost constantly on medium heat for 10 minutes. In a lightly greased 9 x13 Inch baking dish, add the cans of beans, then pour the barbeque sauce over the top; toss to coat evenly. Bake covered for 30 minutes. Remove, stir, and then return back to the stove uncovered for another 30 minutes.

Serves 6

If this picture doesn't make your skin crawl...it's on TOO TIGHT.

Black Christmas

"The sort of Christmas
you don't dream of."

billy's black christmas chili

black christmas

Black Christmas may be one of the best movies that suffered from one of the worst re-makes ever. It's also considered to be the first film to put the terrifying reality of a killer making prank calls from within your house into effect. *Black Christmas* is one of my personal favorites. Now don't get me wrong, I love some gore, but I think one of the reasons I like this movie so much is it doesn't focus too much on over-the-top gore for the sole sake of shock value. At 7 kills, it's still a respectable body count; however, the kills are, dare I say, a bit more poetic. Barb's death by Christmas ornament will always be one of my favorite scenes. I also love the fact that the storyline is great and there are a lot of elements of mystery left to the killer. It's okay Billy, I don't need to know your history; I'll be your Agnes, and we'll make some chili that's killer on all levels. No, for real, I once won a chili cook-off with this recipe. I'll save that story for another time.

ingredients:

Billy's Black Christmas Chili Ingredients:
1 (6 qt) Crock Pot or Slow Cooker
2 lbs Ground Beef
1 Poblano Pepper, Seeded and diced
1 White Onion, Diced
1 Red Pepper, Diced
1 Green Pepper
4 Tomatillos
1 ½ Cups Red Wine, Your favorite Pinot Noir
1 Cup Water
3 Cans Crushed tomatoes, I prefer fire roasted
4 Cloves Garlic, Crushed and diced
2 Cans Black Beans
3 Fresh Bay leaves
1 Teaspoon Red Pepper Flakes
1 Teaspoon Oregano
½ Teaspoon Salt
1 Teaspoon Black Pepper
½ Teaspoon Cumin
1 ½ Teaspoons Pumpkin Pie Seasoning
1 ½ Teaspoons Cinnamon
Salt and Pepper to taste

Agnes's Special Spice ingredients:
2 Tablespoons Cumin
2 Tablespoons Chili Powder
2 Tablespoons Paprika
3 Teaspoons Salt
2 Teaspoons Black Pepper
2 Tablespoons Oregano
2 Teaspoons Sugar
1 Teaspoon Thyme
1 Teaspoon Cinnamon
½ Teaspoon Nutmeg
½ Teaspoon Pumpkin Pie Seasoning

directions:

When I make this chili, I make sure to dice all the veggies super-tiny. I feel like it is a key step that makes all the flavors mesh well together. Cook the ground beef over high heat and with a spatula or spoon, to break up the meat as it cooks. Add the red pepper flakes, oregano, salt, pepper, and cumin; cook until it is browned with no pink left in the meat. Drain the fat and set aside.

Next, add the tomatoes, red wine, and water. Stir to combine, and then add all diced vegetables, garlic, ground beef, bay leaves, cinnamon, and pumpkin pie seasoning. Cover and cook on low heat for 6 hours. Stir occasionally, and add a pinch of salt and pepper every 2 hours. After 6 hours, add the beans, and allow to cook for 30 more minutes. Then, add 4-5 Tablespoons of the spice blend, and ½ teaspoon of Cinnamon. Mix to combine, and then add additional salt and pepper to your liking.

Serves 6-8

"A legend of terror isn't a campfire story anymore!"

cropsy's cream of carrot soup

the burning

The concept of the character Cropsy is based around an urban legend told at summer camps in and around New Jersey and New York. Cropsy was a camp janitor turned garden shear-wielding maniac; he returned to the camp to seek revenge on campers after being severely burned during a prank. Stuff gets real, throats get slashed, and in a famous raft scene, five campers get chopped to bits in a split-second blood bath. *The Burning* constantly gets accused of being a copycat of the more famous Friday the 13th movies. However, writer Harvey Weinstein claims that he actually wrote this film before the release of the first Friday the 13th. It's all a game of "he said, she said" if you ask me, and we should probably just settle these disputes with a cook-off. So Victor Miller, what do you say?

This cream of carrot soup is the only way I will eat blue cheese. The saltiness and sharp flavor of the cheese pairs perfectly with the subtle taste of the carrots. Add a little bacon to the mix, and this is the perfect soup to eat on a cold night around the campfire.

directions:

In a medium-sized skillet over medium heat, cook the bacon. Once the grease begins to the line the pan, add the onions and reduce to a low heat. Cook the bacon until crisp, and sauté the onions for 7 minutes. Remove the bacon and onions and discard the bacon grease. In a large pot over high heat, add the broth, carrots, onion, bacon, rosemary, parsley, salt, pepper and ginger. Bring the mixture to a boil, and then turn your heat down to low. Cover and simmer for 2 hours. With an immersion blender or standard blender, puree the soup until semi-smooth and the carrots are very shredded. Transfer it back to the pot, and add the blue cheese and half and half. Stir until the cheese has melted (about 5 minutes). Add additional salt and pepper to your liking.

Serves 4

Slasher Soups

ingredients:

½ Cup Sweet Onion, chopped
4 Cups Carrots, peeled, thinly sliced
3 Cups Vegetable Broth
1 Cup Water
1 Cup Half and Half Cream
5 Slices of bacon, cooked and crumbled
½ Cup Blue Cheese
½ Teaspoon Ginger Powder
1 Teaspoon Fresh Rosemary

ghost face fiesta soup

scream

Ghost Face came to life in 1996 at the hands of Wes Craven, and who would have guessed what a hit the *Scream* movies would grow to be. *Scream* couldn't have come along at a better time: the slasher genre seemed, well, kind of lifeless. We really were in desperate need of a mask-faced maniac. Ghost Face was that and then some. The one thing I personally really liked about this character was the fact that we not only got a traditional villain, but we got a villain who also has a voice and knows how to use it. If you want to live, just make sure you follow the rules:

You will not survive if you have sex
You will not survive if you drink or do drugs
You will not survive If you say "I'll be right back"
Everyone is a suspect
You will not survive if you ask, "Who's there?"
You will not survive if you go out to investigate a strange noise
You will not survive if you do not make the Ghost Face Fiesta Soup

No, for real...

directions:

In a medium-sized skillet, heat up the olive oil. Add the onion, garlic, jalapeño, and red pepper; sauté for 15 minutes on low heat. In a large pot, add all the ingredients except cheese and cilantro, cover, and bring to a boil. Once a boil is reached, reduce heat to low, and simmer for 2 hours.

In the meantime, to make the tortilla strips: preheat the oven to 375 Degrees. In a small bowl, mix together the olive oil and spices. Gently crush the tortilla chips onto a baking dish. Pour the olive oil mixture over the top and toss to coat. Bake for 10 minutes, and then set aside.

With an immersion blender or by transferring the soup to a blender, mix the soup until it's pureed, then return it back to the pot. Serve with a little cheese, cilantro, and tortilla strips over the top.

Serves 2-3

ingredients:

Ghost Face Fiesta Soup ingredients:
4 Cups Chicken Stock
2 Cups Cauliflower, Chopped
½ White Onion, Chopped
½ Red Pepper, Diced
2 Garlic Cloves, Crushed and diced
2 Tablespoons Jalapeño, Seeded and Diced
2 Tablespoons Olive Oil
½ Cup Black beans
1 Cup Corn
Juice from half a lime
1 Teaspoon Salt
¼ Teaspoon Black Pepper
1 Teaspoon Cumin
½ Teaspoon Cayenne Pepper
¼ Cup Mild Cheddar, to garnish
¼ Cup Cilantro, Chopped to garnish

Craven's Cracked Tortilla Garnish ingredients:
1 Bag Tortilla Chips
3 Tablespoons Olive Oil
1 Teaspoon Chili Powder
½ Teaspoon Garlic Salt

sweet and psycho soup

psycho

Can Alfred Hitchcock do any wrong? *Psycho* inspired many people around the world to be terrified of their showers, and with good reason! This is also another movie that focuses on a man and his mommy issues. After all, "a boy's best friend is his mother." Norman Bates is a man on a mission: a mission to stab pretty women that he is attracted to, because the split personality of his mother is jealous of them. That's normal, right? Although the storyline is semi-typical these days, in 1960 it was a bit harder to come by, which added the extra shock value. Also, Hitchcock does an excellent job at keeping the twist in this movie under wraps, and he really found a gem in Bernard Herrmann as the man behind the music. I strongly believe that *Psycho* wouldn't be the movie it is without the score composed by Herrmann. I'm also a firm believer that winter wouldn't be a manageable season without this comforting winter vegetable soup. It's like the holidays happened in your mouth.

ingredients:

Sweet and Psycho Soup ingredients:
2 Sweet Potatoes, Peeled and chopped
2 Tablespoons Butter
1 Teaspoon Cinnamon
1 Onion, Chopped
1 Cup Squash, Chopped
1 Parsnip, Chopped
3 Garlic Cloves, Diced
1 Tablespoon Jalapeños, Seeded and diced
5 Cups Vegetable Broth
1 Teaspoon Light brown sugar
½ Teaspoon Pumpkin Pie seasoning
1 Teaspoon Salt
1 Teaspoon Black Pepper
½ Teaspoon Cayenne Pepper
½ Teaspoon Paprika

Marion Crane's Caramelized Pumpkin Seeds ingredients:
2 Tablespoons Olive Oil
1 Cup Pumpkin Seeds or Sunflower kernels
½ Teaspoon Light Brown Sugar
1/3 Cup Powdered Sugar

directions:

In a large pot, melt the butter and then add the cinnamon, stirring to combine. Add the onion, garlic, and jalapeños; sauté for 10 minutes on medium heat. Next, add the sweet potatoes, squash, parsnip, and vegetable broth; over high heat, bring the mixture to a boil. Reduce the heat and add all remaining ingredients. Cover and allow to simmer for 1 ½ hours.

In the meantime, to make the pumpkin seeds: heat up the olive oil in a medium-sized skillet. Sauté the pumpkin seeds or sunflower kernels in the oil for 2 minutes. Add the powdered sugar and brown sugar, and cook until a caramel-like substance begins to appear. The pumpkin seeds will become gooey and delicious. Remove from the heat and set aside.

Transfer the soup mixture to a blender, and puree it until smooth. Return it back to the pot, and season the soup with additional salt and pepper to your liking. Serve garnished with some caramelized seeds.

Serves 4-6

They were warned... They are doomed...
And on Friday the 13th, nothing will save them.

FRIDAY THE 13TH

A 24 hour nightmare of terror

"*Lucky 13? I think not.*"

vengeful voorhees' vegetable soup

friday the 13th

Ah, the story of a man in a mask, with a machete, who likes to terrorize the young counselors of Camp Crystal Lake. If Jason taught you anything, it's to not have sex in the woods. I, on the other hand, will just write that off as "don't even sleep in the woods." The further I'm getting into writing this cookbook, the more I'm realizing that most of my neuroses come from watching too many horror movies. *Friday the 13th* is often thought of as the rip-off of *Halloween*, and writer Victor Miller has openly stated that he "purposely rode the success of Carpenter's Halloween." I guess you can't really fault a guy who saw an opportunity and went for it. What I can fault him for is putting Jason in a frickin' spaceship in Jason X! Really?! What were you thinking? This Vengeful Voorhees soup is light on the stomach, but slaughters in the flavor department. It's the perfect alternative to a chicken noodle soup.

directions:

In a large pot, heat the olive oil over medium heat. Add the celery, onion, and garlic. Sauté for 8 minutes, but do not brown. Next, add the broth and bring it to a boil over high heat. Reduce to low heat and add the remaining ingredients. Cover and simmer for 4 hours, stirring occasionally. At the 2-hour mark, add the lemon juice. Add additional salt and pepper to your liking.

Serves 2-3

ingredients:

5 Cups Vegetable Broth
1/3 Cup Broccoli, Diced
2 Celery Stalks Diced
¼ Cup leaves from celery stalks, Diced
1/3 Cup Carrots, Thinly shredded
½ Yellow Onion, Chopped
3 Garlic Cloves, Crushed and diced
½ Cup Cabbage, Chopped
½ Cup Baby Corn
¼ Cup Peas
2 Tablespoons Olive Oil
1 Teaspoon Salt
1 Teaspoon Pepper
1 Tablespoon Lemon Juice

"For God's sake, get out!"

amityville angel hair

amityville horror

I remember the first time I saw *The Amityville Horror*. I instantly got up as the credits started rolling and glued my face to the computer as I tried to research everything about said "true events." Some of you might think that's nerditry to the 10th power, but to me that's everyday life. *The Amityville Horror* is rumored to be based on a true story surrounding a large, possessed house on the coast of Long Island and the Lutz family whom, at the time, occupied it. When are people going to learn that when someone "warns" you about a house's freaky history, the wrong process of thinking is "houses don't have memories?" I believe that there are at least 100 movies that circle around that concept. Unfortunately, in this case, it isn't George Lutz's lucky day. The evil in the house sticks it's claws into him, forcing George to become erratic, angry, and dangerous. Regardless if this story is truth or a hoax, it has taught me to be terrified of any child with an imaginary friend. Also, that the remake should have really been titled The Amityville Horror: The Ryan Reynolds No-Shirt Edition.

This lightweight lemon pasta is perfect for a summer picnic, or a good base for adding other meats and vegetables. I personally like the simplicity of it as it, but it also pairs perfectly with grilled chicken or shrimp.

directions:

Preheat oven to 400 Degrees. In a medium-sized bowl, mix together the chopped asparagus with the olive oil and balsamic vinegar. Place the coated asparagus on a baking sheet and sprinkle with salt, pepper, and garlic. Bake for 8 minutes, or until bright green and tender.

In a large saucepan over high heat, bring the water to a boil. Stir in the pasta and cook for 4 minutes or until tender. In the meantime, in a small bowl mix together all the remaining ingredients except the basil and parmesan. Drain the pasta, and then pour the lemon mixture into the pasta. Add the baked asparagus and parmesan, and toss to completely coat the pasta. Served garnished with fresh basil.

Serves 2-3

ingredients:

Amityville Angel Hair ingredients:
8 Ounces Angel Hair pasta
1 Lemon juiced
½ Cup Olive Oil
½ Cup Parmesan Cheese, grated
1 Tablespoon Butter, melted
1 Tablespoon Minced Garlic
1 Tablespoon Fresh Chives, diced
½ Teaspoon Teaspoon Black Pepper
1 ½ Teaspoon Red Pepper Flakes
½ Teaspoon Salt
Fresh Basil to garnish

Father Bolen's Baked Asparagus ingredients:
1 Cup Asparagus, chopped
2 Tablespoons Olive Oil
1 Tablespoon Balsamic Vinegar
Pinch of Salt, Black Pepper, Garlic Powder

baked spaghetti sematary

pet sematary

Pet Sematary gets a lot of flak from people for what I see as no good reason. I happen to really love this movie. Who knows, maybe I'm biased to the fact that an oddly-adorable yet evil cat runs rampant through the movie, and if given the chance I'd be the cat woman from *The Simpsons* in a heartbeat. Regardless, it's great to see a visually-stunning and well-executed movie come from a woman director. Mary Lambert does a fantastic job in what is predominantly a "sausage fest" type of work environment. She had particularly big shoes to fill, considering George Romero was originally set to direct this film before dropping out due to filming delays. It's also said that Stephen King was quite difficult on Lambert, and even spent a ton of time on set making sure his screenplay was rigorously followed. Now if you still hate this movie, can we at least agree that the character of Zelda was absolutely frightening? I'm pretty sure I peed my pants the first, second, and possibly third times I saw the famous bedroom scene. Is talking about peeing one's pants in a cookbook in bad taste? Food, ah yes, let's talk about food. This baked spaghetti gives a new twist to the classic spaghetti dish. It is kind of a hybrid of spaghetti and lasagna, and has everything you could love about Italian flavors in forkfuls of bliss.

directions:

In a large saucepan, mix together all the pasta sauce ingredients. Over high heat, bring it to a boil. Reduce to low heat and let simmer, covered, for 2 hours, stirring occasionally. In a medium-sized skillet over high heat, cook the ground beef. Crumble the meat as you cook, and also add the red pepper flakes, onion powder, and seasoning salt. Cook until there is no pink left in the meat, and then drain the fat from the meat. Transfer the cooked ground beef to the sauce, and then continue to let simmer for 15 minutes.

Preheat oven to 350 Degrees. Cook the pasta according to the manufacturer's directions, then set it aside. In a 13 x 9 x 2-inch baking dish, layer the bottom with a little bit of sauce. Next, layer with half of the spaghetti, followed by half of the sauce, and the ricotta. Repeat the layers, except use the pepper jack in this next rotation instead of ricotta. Cover and bake in the oven for 45 minutes.

Serves 8-10

ingredients:

Baked Spaghetti Sematary ingredients:
1 lb Spaghetti
1 (15 ounce) Ricotta Cheese
4 Cups Pepper Jack Cheese, shredded
1 lb Ground Beef
1 Teaspoon Red Pepper Flakes
1 Teaspoon Onion Powder
1 Teaspoon Seasoning Salt

Zelda's Petrifying Pasta Sauce ingredients:
1 (28 ounce) Can Crushed tomatoes
1 (28 ounce) Can Tomato Sauce
1 Cup Water
½ Cup Dry Red wine
½ Cup White onion, Diced
½ Cup Green Pepper, Diced
2 Celery Stalks, Diced
4 Cloves Garlic, Crushed and Diced
1 Fresh Bay Leaf
2 Fresh Basil Leaves
2 Fresh Thyme leaves
1 Teaspoon Salt
1 Teaspoon Sugar
1 ½ Teaspoon Black Pepper
1 ½ Teaspoon Italian Seasoning
½ Teaspoon Rosemary

"You may not believe in ghosts but you cannot deny terror."

hill house spicy spaghetti

the haunting

Tons of people want to prove ghosts exist, and Dr. Markway is no exception. However, he will soon find out that he may have bitten off more than he can chew with the eerie mansion filled with violent death and insanity, Hill House. *The Haunting* (1963) consists of beautiful cinematography with a genuine tone of underlying terror without having to be too bedazzled. There is no gore or maniacal killer, but there is an element that is more terrifying then both of those things: the sheer terror of what goes on in a person's mind, and how a movie can psychologically affect an audience. *The Haunting* is an under-rated classic movie that all of you should run out and watch now if you haven't already. Then come home and cook this classic spaghetti and meatball dish, and focus on the fact that your gore will come in the form of tomatoes tonight.

ingredients:

Hill House Spicy Spaghetti ingredients:
1 lb Spaghetti
1 (28 oz) Can Crushed Tomatoes
1 (15 oz) Can Tomato Sauce
1 (6 oz) Can Tomato Paste
1/3 Cup Red Wine
½ Cup Water
2 Tablespoons Olive oil
4 Garlic cloves, crushed and diced
½ Cup Yellow Onion, diced
2 Fresh Basil leaves
2 Tablespoons Fresh Parsley, diced
1 Teaspoon Italian Seasoning
1 Teaspoon Salt
1 Teaspoon Sugar
1 Teaspoon Red Pepper flakes
½ Teaspoon Black Pepper
½ Teaspoon Cinnamon
½ Teaspoon Oregano
½ Teaspoon Chili Powder
1 Cup Parmesan cheese to garnish

Dr. Markway's Meatballs ingredients:
1 lb Ground Beef
½ lb Ground Pork
½ Cup Italian Style Bread crumbs
1/3 Cup Milk
2 Eggs
½ Cup Parmesan Cheese, grated
1 Tablespoon Fresh Parsley, diced
2 Tablespoons Minced Garlic
1 Tablespoon Onion Powder
½ Teaspoon Salt
½ Teaspoon Black Pepper

directions:

In a large saucepan, heat up the olive oil. Add the onion and garlic and sauté for 5 minutes. Next, add the crushed tomatoes, tomato sauce, tomato paste, wine, and water. Bring to a boil over high heat. Reduce to low heat and add the remainder of the ingredients, except for the cheese. Cover and let simmer for 3 hours. In the meantime, prepare the meatballs.

Preheat oven to 400 Degrees. In a large bowl, combine the beef and pork. Add the eggs, cheese, parsley, garlic, onion, salt, and pepper. Next, mix the breadcrumbs into the mixture. Slowly mix in the milk, and then form the concoction into the shape of meatballs. Place the meatballs in a lightly greased baking dish and bake for 25-30 minutes. Make sure to rotate the meatballs halfway through.

At the 4 hour mark, add the meatballs to the sauce mixture and continue to simmer for the next hour. Cook the pasta according to the manufacturer's instructions. Serve the pasta with sauce poured over, meatballs, and a little parmesan to top.

Serves 4-6

paranormal alfredo 2

paranormal activity 2

I'm not going to lie, when I initially saw the first *Paranormal Activity* film I wasn't overly impressed. Maybe I expected to much out of it due to all the hype. After all, it is a well-known fact that a handful of my male friends had sleepless nights after watching it. Needless to say, when the news of the 2nd film came out I wasn't overly enthused. Boy, did I eat a big bowl of crow on that one! *Paranormal Activity 2* is one of the best sequels I have ever seen. The way it fills in all the blanks of the first movie and manages to tie the past with the present is fantastic. I'm getting excited about it all over again just thinking about it! Just don't you dare walk in my house with a video camera from this point on, or we're going to have problems.

I love a good Alfredo. However, just like movies, many restaurants have a hard time making them. They're usually soaked in oil, watered-down, and very bland in the flavor department. It's a crime against humanity, I tell you. This Alfredo recipe has a bold, rich flavor, and it balances out the creaminess of an Alfredo sauce with the heartiness of chicken and the light taste of broccoli.

ingredients:

Paranormal Alfredo 2 ingredients:
1 lb Fettuccini
2 Cups Heavy Cream
1 ½ Cups Parmesan Cheese, grated
4 Ounces Cream Cheese
3 Garlic Cloves Crushed
1/3 Cup White Onion, diced
¼ Cup Fresh Basil, diced
2 Tablespoons Butter
½ Teaspoon Lemon Juice
1 Teaspoon Parsley
1 Teaspoon Black Pepper
1 Teaspoon Garlic Powder
½ Teaspoon Thyme
½ Teaspoon Oregano
½ Teaspoon Rosemary
½ Teaspoon Salt
½ Teaspoon Crushed Red Pepper
1 Cup Broccoli, Chopped and stems discarded

Cursed Chicken ingredients:
4 Chicken Breast, Boneless and skinless
1 Bottle Italian Dressing

directions:

Trim any excess fat off the chicken, and then place it in a container. Make small jabs into the chicken using a knife. Next, pour the bottle of dressing over the chicken. Toss to coat, and then cover. Refrigerate for 2 hours.

Preheat oven to 350 Degrees. Place the chicken in a baking dish, and cook for 40-45 minutes or until no longer pink. Melt the butter in a large saucepan over high heat. Add the onion and garlic, and continue to sauté over medium heat for 10 minutes. Next, add the heavy cream and bring the mixture to a boil. Reduce the heat to low, add the remainder of ingredients except the broccoli, cheese, and fettuccine. Continue to cook the cream over medium heat, mixing occasionally for another 5 minutes.

In the meantime, cook the broccoli by filling a small saucepan with 2 Cups of water. Bring the water to a boil, and then add the broccoli. Cook for 5 minutes, or until desired softness. Strain the broccoli, and then add it to the Alfredo sauce. Toss to fully coat the broccoli. Lastly, add the cheese and bring the mixture to a boil over medium-high heat. Stir constantly until the mixture begins to thicken (about 8-10 minutes).

Cook the fettuccine according to the manufacturer's directions; drain it and transfer it to the Alfredo sauce. Toss to completely coat all the noodles. Add additional salt and pepper to your liking and serve with the chopped chicken over the top.

Serves 6

"Some things have to be believed to be seen."

poltergeist penne

poltergeist

I may or may not have watched this movie multiple times in a hand-made fort well into my adult years. And by "may or may not," I mean I definitely have. No shame. *Poltergeist* may be the scariest film ever that contains no casualties. Well, unless you count the dead bird. Unfortunately, in real life this wasn't the case, as two of the leading young stars died shortly after the movie was released in 1982. The teenage daughter Dana, played by Dominique Dunne, died November 4th, 1982 at the age of 23 by being violently choked to death by her ex-boyfriend (she ultimately succumbed to brain damage). Subsequently, the movie's star that played Carol Anne, Heather O'Rourke, died in 1988 at the young age of 12 due to cardiopulmonary arrest and intestinal stenosis. Well, now that I just bummed everyone out, let's build a fort, watch a great ghost story, and eat some spicy chicken sausage and penne pasta in their honor.

ingredients:

Poltergeist Penne ingredients:
1 (15 ounce) Box Penne pasta
4 Spicy Chicken Sausages, diced up
2 Tablespoons Olive Oil to fry
1/3 Cup Grape tomatoes, halved
1 (15 oz) Can Tomato sauce
1 (6 oz) Can Tomato Paste with Basil, Garlic, and Oregano
1 Tablespoon Minced Garlic
1 Cup Dry White Wine
1 ½ Cups water
¼ Cup Pesto
1 Tablespoon Olive oil
1 Teaspoon Onion Powder
½ Teaspoon Oregano
½ Teaspoon Black pepper
½ Teaspoon Sugar
¼ Teaspoon Thyme
¼ Teaspoon Rosemary
¼ Teaspoon Salt

Supernatural Sautéed Spinach ingredients:
2 Cups Baby Spinach leaves
¼ Cup Yellow Onion, diced
2 Tablespoons Olive oil
½ Teaspoon Salt
¼ Teaspoon Black Pepper

directions:

In a medium skillet, heat the olive oil over high heat. Dice the sausage and then cook it until browned. Drain the grease and then set the meat aside. In a large saucepan over high heat, place the remainder of ingredients, except the penne, and bring to a boil. Reduce the heat to low and add the cooked sausage. Cover partially and cook for 1 hour, stirring occasionally.

When there is 30 minutes left on the sauce, it's time to sauté the spinach. Heat the olive oil in a small-sized saucepan over medium heat. Add the onion; reduce to a low heat and sauté for 5 minutes. Next, add the spinach, salt, and pepper. Toss to coat, and then cover and cook for 5 minutes. Uncover the pot, and cook for another 2 minutes, stirring constantly, and then transfer to the sauce mixture.

Cook the pasta according to the manufacturer's instructions, and then drain. Add the cooked pasta to the sauce, and toss to completely coat.

Serves 4

"When there's no more room in Hell, the dead will walk the Earth."

breakfast of the dead pizza

dawn of the dead

Does George Romero do any wrong with zombie movies? Scratch that, did George Romero do any wrong with his early zombie movies? That would be a no. *Dawn of the Dead* was the second and most profitable film of the "Dead" series. I partially believe it was so successful because it takes place in a mall and has zombies (duh), but also because it has a pretty gnarly militant biker gang. I like to think that in another life I was in a biker gang; realistically that's probably false because I can barely even walk straight. Coordination was never my best suit. There has been a lot of dispute to the possible idea of an alternate ending to *Dawn of the Dead*. Some people on set claim there was an ending shot were both Peter and Fran kill themselves. For years Romero denied these allegations, however, during the documentary *Document of the Dead* he clearly states there was, in fact, an alternate ending shot, but the effects weren't done. Regardless, I like to think that Romero released the ending he did because he knew Peter and Fran wanted to live to see another morning so they could dine on the "Breakfast of the Dead" pizza.

directions:

Preheat oven to 425 Degrees. On a pizza tray with vent holes, roll out the crescent roll. On the tray, lay the crescent rolls out vertically forming 2 rectangles. With your fingers, pinch together all the precut spots making it one big smooth square of dough. Start with a layer of cut sausage, and follow with the prosciutto and cheese. In the center of the pizza towards both ends, with a spoon make a small indent hole. Make sure to only go as deep as the toppings, and not go through the dough. Crack the eggs in the two pre-made indents, and then sprinkle with the chives, salt, and pepper. Bake for 18 minutes, or until crust is golden and egg has cooked. Before you serve the pizza, make sure to take a fork to the egg yolk, break it, and allow it to run all over the pizza.

Serves 2

Zombie Plagued Pizzas

ingredients:

4 Prosciutto slices
4 Mini Pre-cooked Sausage links, diced
2 Eggs
1 Cup Mild Cheddar, Shredded
1 Package Crescent rolls
1 Tablespoon Fresh Chives, diced
Salt and Pepper to taste

ZOMBIES, GUNS AND SEX, OH MY!

RUPERT EVERETT
FRANÇOIS HADJI-LAZARO
ANNA FALCHI

CEMETERY MAN

a film by
MICHELE SOAVI

GIANNI ROMOLI   CONCHITA AIROLDI   and DINO DI DIONISIO

TILDE CORSI GIANNI ROMOLI MICHELE SOAVI

"Zombies, guns, and sex, oh my!"

cemetery man pizza dough

the beyond

Cemetery Man is somewhat of an odd movie that people tend to either love or hate. I can understand why people have such mixed feelings towards this film. At times it doesn't seem to know what it wants to be as it bounces between horror, comedy, and art flick. At times it is a bit bipolar, but all in all, I think Director Michele Soavi does a great job at making all these genres blend well together. Now, I'm very aware that I have weird "ticks;" I am the person who will go out of their way to a branch of a food place just because their location has crispier fries. My "tick" with *Cemetery Man* has always been that I can't get over the fact that Christopher Walken doesn't play the lead character, Franesco Dellamorte. There is just something about every inch of my soul that believes that's the way this movie should have gone. I told you I was odd, but come on; I'm pairing the undead with food right now, so you should have seen that coming. I dare you all to give *Cemetery Man* another watch, but instead imagine Walken in the place of Rupert Everett; you'll be doing the Walken dance afterwards too. Just make sure to save time to do the pizza dough dance with this easy and versatile recipe.

ingredients:

1 ¾ Cups Warm water
1 (1/4-ounce) Package Active Dry Yeast
3 ½ Cups Bread Flour
8 Tablespoons Olive oil
1 Tablespoon Sugar
1 Tablespoon Honey
1 Teaspoon Garlic Powder
1 Teaspoon Italian Seasoning
1 Teaspoon Onion Powder

directions:

In a small bowl, activate the yeast by mixing the warm water with it. Allow to sit for 15 minutes. In the meantime, in a blender or large food processor, add 1 cup of flour, sugar, garlic, Italian seasoning, and onion powder. Pulse 4 times to blend. Next, add the yeast and water mixture, and pulse 5 times. Add 4 tablespoons olive oil and the honey, followed by the remaining flour. Mix until well blended, occasionally stopping to scrape down the sides.

Remove dough; on a very well-floured surface, knead it until smooth (about 8 minutes). Grease a large bowl with 4 tablespoons of olive oil. Place the dough into the bowl, and turn to coat all sides. Cover the bowl tightly with a damp cloth and place in a warm area for about 45 minutes. This will allow the dough to rise and double in size.

Once the dough has risen, punch it down and allow it to rest for 10 minutes. Split the dough in half, and each half will make 1 10-12 inch pizza. If you don't need the second part of the dough, it will freeze perfectly; just place it in a sealable bag and store it in the freezer. Just make sure that when you're ready to use it, you transfer the dough to the refrigerator to thaw 24 hours before use.

Makes 2

Zombie Plagued Pizzas

YOU'RE INVITED
TO ORVILLE'S "COMING-OUT" PARTY...

It'll Be A Scream   ...YOURS!!

P.S. CHILDREN SHOULDN'T
PLAY WITH
DEAD THINGS!

A BENJAMIN CLARK FILM
STARRING ALAN ORMSBY · JANE DALY · ANYA ORMSBY · JEFFREY GILLEN
VALERIE MAMCHES · PAUL CRONIN — SETH SKLAREY
PRODUCED BY BENJAMIN CLARK & GARY GOCH
MUSIC BY CARL ZITTRER · WRITTEN & DIRECTED BY BENJAMIN CLARK
RELEASED THRU GEMINI FILM DISTRIBUTORS

PG

"Experience the unexpected
terror of rising, rotting flesh."

children shouldn't play with veg things pizza

children shouldn't play with dead things

Children Shouldn't Play with Dead Things teaches us valuable life lessons, such as, don't piss off the dead. This is an under-rated movie by a great director. Bob Clark, more famous for directing *Black Christmas* and *A Christmas Story*, does a great job at making a fun zombie movie on an extremely low budget. The only truly unfortunate thing is the fact that, amongst plans to remake this film in 2007, he unexpectedly passed away due to a head-on car accident at the hands of a drunk driver. Yes, at times *Children Shouldn't Play with Dead Things* moves at a slow pace, is heavily influenced by Romero films, and leaves you wondering when the zombies are coming. However, this is a great B-movie for anyone who understands and enjoys the allure and atmosphere that was '70s horror. Still not your cup of tea? At least you learn to leave satanic rituals and borderline-necrophilia gags to the professionals.

This veggie Alfredo pizza has everything I could want out of food. It's a great alternative to your everyday red sauce pizza, simple in ingredients, and could raise the dead with flavor.

ingredients:

Alan's Alfredo ingredients:
2 Tablespoons Butter
½ Cup Cream Cheese
2 Teaspoons Minced Garlic
1 Cup Heavy Cream
1 Tablespoon All-purpose Flour
½ Cup Parmesan Cheese
½ Cup Mozzarella Cheese
½ Teaspoon Black Pepper
½ Teaspoon Salt

Children Shouldn't Play with Veg Things pizza ingredients:
½ Cup Red Onion, chopped
½ Cup Green Pepper, chopped
¼ Cup Black Olives, sliced
¼ Cup Zucchini, diced
2 Cups Mozzarella Cheese
Pizza Dough or 1 Pre-made pizza crust

directions:

Preheat oven to 450 Degrees. In a small sauce pan over medium heat, melt the butter. Over high heat, add the heavy cream and bring the mixture to a boil. Reduce back to a medium heat, and then add the remainder of ingredients, except the flour. Stir until all the cheeses melt, and then add the flour. Mix until the flour has dissolved and the mixture thickens (about 3 minutes).

Spoon 9 Tablespoons of the Alfredo sauce over the pizza crust, followed by all the veggies, and then top it off with the cheese. Bake for 15-20 minutes or until the crust has browned. If using premade crust, bake according to manufacturer's directions.

Serves 4-6

Zombie Plagued Pizzas

"EIN! ZWEI! DIE!"

dead snow siesta fiesta pizza

dead snow

I don't want to say *Dead Snow* revolutionized the zombie movie; however, it definitely gave us a new twist on the genre. Let's face it: in 2009, the idea of a good zombie film was somewhat on life support. During what I like to refer to as the "dark days," Norwegian director Tommy Wirkola did everyone a "solid" and came through with a home run of a film. *Dead Snow* goes to a place no other horror film to my recollection goes to: Nazi Zombies. Wirkola gives a nice slapstick kind of tone to this movie and also pays homage to the *Evil Dead* franchise at many points. All in all, we have a blast of a film that is a perfect no-brainer for the viewer, and on top of that, it manages to perfectly pair horror and humor without the over-the-top special effects and too much corniness. Unfortunately for the vacationers in the film, their siesta turned more into a fiesta with zombies. You should probably make this taco pizza and see if you have better luck.

ingredients:

½ (16 Ounce) Can Refried Beans
1 (6 Ounce) can Tomato Paste
4 Tablespoons Salsa
2 Cups Mild Cheddar Cheese, shredded
1 Cup Lettuce, Chopped
½ Cup White Onion, diced
½ Pound Ground Beef
1 Bag Cool Ranch Doritos
1 Pouch Taco Seasoning
½ Teaspoon Chili Powder
½ Teaspoon Cumin
½ Teaspoon Onion Powder
1 Teaspoon Minced Garlic
1 Tablespoon Jalapeño, Seeded and diced
Sour Cream, optional
Pizza Dough Recipe or 1 Pre-made Pizza Crust

directions:

Preheat oven to 450 Degrees. In a small bowl, mix together the beans, onion, and salsa. In another medium-sized bowl, mix the tomato paste with 2 Teaspoons of water to dilute it down. Next, add the chili powder, cumin, onion powder, and minced garlic. Mix to completely combine, and then set aside. In a large skillet, begin to cook the ground beef. Add ½ the pouch of taco seasoning and the jalapeños. Cook until the meat is browned and no longer pink. Drain the grease, and then transfer the meat mixture to the bowl of tomato paste and mix to combine.

You can use any dough that you'd like for the pizza crust, whether it be our *Cemetery Man* recipe or something else. Assemble the pizza by first spreading the bean mixture on the dough, followed by the ground beef, and then the cheese. Cook for 15-20 minutes, or until crust is browned. Once out of the oven, put on the chopped lettuce followed by a generous amount of crushed Doritos. Serve with sour cream on top if you like. If using premade crust, bake according to manufacturer's directions.

Serves 4-6

"Your tearing flesh will scream for death!"

let southwestern corpse burgers lie pizza

let sleeping corpses lie

Let Sleeping Corpses Lie is an unfairly ignored movie. It's witty, imaginative, stylish, and when the zombies hit, they hit hard. In a similar fashion to Romero's *Night of the Living Dead*, Jorge Grau's zombies also rise due to suspected radiation. I think we're beginning to see a theme here. Although there are some similarities in how the dead rose, I wouldn't say this film was a rip-off by any means. Plus, *Let Sleeping Corpses Lie* also has hippies, maniac babies, and a boob grabbing scene that will make you cringe to the core. The only thing that could make any of these scenes better is eating them with this southwestern burger that is conveniently in pizza form.

ingredients:

Pizza Dough recipe or Pre-made Pizza Crust
½ Cup Onion, diced
5 Tablespoons BBQ Sauce
2 Tablespoons Ranch Dressing
½ Pound Ground Beef
1 Tablespoon Jalapeño, Seeded and diced
2 Tablespoons Salsa
1 Teaspoon Grill Master Smokey Mesquite Seasoning
11 Pieces of Bacon, Cooked
2 Cups Colby Jack Cheese, shredded

directions:

Preheat oven to 450 Degrees. In a medium-sized skillet over high heat, cook the ground beef with the jalapeños, onion, and mesquite seasoning until meat is browned and no longer pink. Drain the grease and then transfer the cooked meat to a medium-sized bowl and mix with the salsa. Next, cook the bacon in a medium skillet until brown and crunchy. Set aside.

In a small bowl, mix together the BBQ sauce and ranch dressing. To assemble the pizza, spread the BBQ sauce mixture over the dough. Follow with the ground beef, strips of bacon, and then the cheese. Cook for 15-20 minutes or until crust is golden brown. Eat as is, or top with some sour cream or lettuce and tomatoes. If using premade crust, bake according to manufacturer's directions.

Serves 4-6

Zombie Plagued Pizzas

"They keep coming back in a bloodthirsty lust for HUMAN FLESH!"

night of the thanksliving day pizza

night of the living dead

Let's face it: this is one of the best horror movies ever made. *Night of the Living Dead* was George Romero's film debut, and a shocking success. Coming out at

a time when the movie industry was drastically changing, there's a lot to say about a movie that held on to old characteristics (such as being a black-and-white film) and still did so well. Radiation from a fallen satellite may be the cause for the disturbing resurfacing of the dead ready to dine on the living for food. What I personally think is cool is the fact that, at the time this film was made, said flesh-eating beasts weren't even referred to as zombies yet. Throughout the whole movie, these gnarly grave-risers were only known as "things" or "ghouls." *Night of the Living Dead* is a perfect example of a cult classic, and an inspirational gateway guideline for many horror movies over the decades.

Thanksgiving was an inspirational gateway guideline for my next pizza recipe. This circle of creativity helps you enjoy the gluttony goodness of the holidays year round. It also is the perfect option for all your seasonal leftovers when you're looking for other ways to keep the feeding frenzy going.

ingredients:

Barbra's Biscuit Crust ingredients:
2 Cups All-purpose flour
1 Cup Bread flour
1 Tablespoon Baking Powder
½ Cup Butter
¾ cup Butter Milk
1 Teaspoon Minced Garlic
1 Teaspoon Honey
½ Teaspoon Salt

Radiation Mashed Potatoes ingredients:
2 Pounds Baking Potatoes, peeled and quartered
2 Tablespoons Butter
¼ Cup Heavy Cream
2 Tablespoons Fresh Chives, diced
6 Garlic cloves, peeled
1/3 Cup Cream Cheese, softened
Salt and Pepper to taste

Farmhouse Gravy ingredients:
2 ½ Cups Chicken Broth
2 Teaspoons Chicken Bouillon Granules
½ Cup Milk
¼ Cup All-Purpose Flour
½ Onion, Roughly chopped
1 Teaspoon Gravy Master browning sauce
¼ Teaspoon Black Pepper

Survival Stuffing ingredients:
¼ Cup Butter
10 Cups Dried Unseasoned Bread cubes
1 White Onion, diced
2 Celery Stalks, diced
2 Eggs, beaten
2 Cups Chicken Stock
2 Tablespoons Fresh Parsley, chopped
1 Teaspoon Minced Garlic
1 Teaspoon Fresh Thyme, diced
1 Teaspoon Fresh Sage, diced
½ Teaspoon Fresh Rosemary
¼ Teaspoon Salt
½ Teaspoon Black Pepper

Night of the Thanksliving Day Pizza Ingredients:
2 Cups Premade store bought Turkey
Fresh Chives, chopped
Pinch of Black Pepper

directions:

Barbara's Biscuit Crust: In a large mixing bowl sift together both flours, baking powder, and salt. Mix in butter until the consistency resembles crumbs. Pour in milk, garlic, honey, and mix until dough becomes soft and pliable. Place dough onto a lightly floured surface and knead until it is no longer sticky, about 8 minutes. Add additional flour if needed. Roll dough out on a pizza dish with vent holes, leaving it about 1 inch thick. Set aside.

Radiated Mashed Potatoes: In a large saucepan bring water to a boil over high heat. Add whole garlic cloves and the potatoes. Cover and allow to cook for 20 minutes or until potatoes have softened. Drain water, and discard garlic cloves. In a small saucepan over low heat, heat butter, cream cheese, and heavy cream until butter has fully melted. Transfer the butter, cream cheese, and heavy cream to the potatoes and mash together until it becomes smooth and creamy. Add the fresh chives, and salt and pepper to liking.

Continued on page 108

Zombie Plagued Pizzas

"The most controversial movie ever made"

cannibal holowraps

cannibal holocaust

Cannibal Holocaust might be the craziest movie ever made. Shortly after this movie first premiered in Milan, many rumors started swirling that it was in fact a snuff film and not fictional. The Italian courts eventually seized the film, and director Ruggero Deodato was arrested on charges of obscenity and murder. Luckily, everything was soon straightened out and Deodato managed to dodge life in prison. Nonetheless, *Cannibal Holocaust* remained banned in Italy for another three years, and is reportedly banned in over 50 countries worldwide as well. Although not controversial, these chicken wraps will still make you want to impale someone with a stick and rip out an unborn fetus. Just don't forget the spicy mayo…oh, how I love cannibal movies!

ingredients:

Cannibal Holowraps ingredients:
1 (15 ounce) Package Chicken strips
1 Package Large Flour Tortillas
½ Cup Mild Cheddar
Lettuce, Chopped
1 Tablespoon Olive Oil

Professor Monroe's Chicken Marinade ingredients:
½ Cup Tequilla
½ Cup Lime Juice
2 Tablespoons Chili Sauce
1 Tablespoon Fresh Chives, diced
1 Teaspoon Garlic Powder
½ Teaspoon Red Pepper flakes
½ Teaspoon Black Pepper
¼ Teaspoon salt

The Yanomanos Mayonnaise ingredients:
½ Cup Mayo
1 Tablespoon Canned Green Chilies, diced
1 Tablespoon and 1 Teaspoon White Onion, diced
1 Tablespoon Tomato, diced
1 Teaspoon Garlic, minced
½ Teaspoon Cayenne pepper
½ Teaspoon Black Pepper
¼ Teaspoon Salt
¼ Cumin

directions:

In a medium-sized bowl, mix together all the marinade ingredients. Add the chicken to the marinade, and then toss to completely coat. Cover and allow to sit for 2 hours. In a small bowl, mix together all the mayonnaise ingredients; cover and chill for one hour. After 2 hours, heat up the olive oil in a large skillet over medium-high heat. Add the chicken and fry until cooked, about 4-5 minutes. In a medium-sized skillet on low heat, place one tortilla with a generous amount of cheese sprinkled on top of the whole perimeter. Allow the cheese to melt, and then place a comfortable amount of chicken in the center, followed by a tablespoon of spicy mayo; top it off with a little lettuce. Fold both ends of the tortilla towards the center, and then roll the shell so it forms a wrap. Turn the wrap folded-side down, and heat for another 10 seconds. Repeat all steps with the other tortillas.

Makes 3

"In their world adults are
not allowed...to live."

children of the chicken

children of the corn

Hear ye, here ye: if you are over the age of 17, it's time to fear "he who walks behind the rows." Unfortunately, we don't fully know who "he who walks behind the rows" is, but he seems to have quite a hold over the corn and the children of Gatlin. Sorry adults, you're cut off, literally. *Children of the Corn* is another well-known Stephen King movie that people seem to either love or hate. I love the concept of this movie, because I could kind of see something like this happening somewhere. What I do have a hard time with, though, is the chosen ending. I for one do not watch horror movies for "happy endings," and the fact that the movie's "powers-that-be" decided to cut King's original, quite brutal ending is just silly to me! In the short story, "the thing" kills Burt shortly after he finds his wife crucified. Not only was she crucified, but also her eyes were plucked out and the empty sockets filled with cornhusks. So…why was this cut? That's like paying for the buffet and not going back for seconds. Now I'm just getting myself all worked up and I have the urge to write hate mail. This Children of the Chicken recipe has the perfect combo of spicy and sweet, and pairs perfectly with this easy egg-fried rice. If you don't agree, I guess I'll allow hate mail too.

ingredients:

Children of the Chicken ingredients:
½ White Onion, roughly chopped
1 Jalapeño, sliced vertically and seeded
1 Ginger root, Medium sized and peeled
2 Cloves of Garlic, peeled and cut in half
½ Red Pepper, roughly chopped
½ Cup Soy Sauce
2 Tablespoons Orange Juice
¼ Cup Sugar
¼ Cup Chili Sauce
2 Tablespoons Rice Vinegar
1 Tablespoon Cornstarch
1/3 Cup Corn, drained
1 Tablespoon Olive Oil
3 Chicken Breasts, boneless, skinless, and fat trimmed

Gatlin Garlic Rice ingredients:
Generous 1 Cup White Rice
2 Tablespoons Light Olive oil
2 Tablespoons Minced Garlic
2 Eggs, beaten
2 Tablespoons Parsley, diced
2 Tablespoons Soy Sauce
1 Teaspoon Fresh Rosemary
¼ Teaspoon Chili Powder
¼ Teaspoon Saffron

directions:

Preheat oven to 350 Degrees. Combine ½ Cup water with the soy sauce in a small saucepan over high heat. After the mixture comes to a boil, add the onion, ginger, garlic, jalapeño, and red pepper. Bring the mixture to a boil and then lower the heat, cover the pan, and simmer for 20 minutes. Next, strain out the vegetables and return the sauce mixture to the pan over low heat. Discard the vegetables.

Add the orange juice, sugar, chili sauce, and vinegar; continue to cook on low heat. In the meantime, in a small skillet, heat up the olive oil. Once warm, add the corn and sauté for 6 minutes over medium heat; be careful not to burn the corn. Transfer the corn over to the liquid mixture and continue to cook on low heat. In a small bowl, mix the cornstarch with 2 Tablespoons of water. Make sure that the consistency is lump-free and smooth. Remove the sauce mixture from the heat, add the cornstarch, and then put it back on the heat. Bring the mixture to a boil, and stir constantly for 1 minute, or until sauce thickens. If you want to adjust the consistency of the glaze to your liking, mix in more water, adding only 1 Tablespoon at a time.

Place the chicken in a lightly-greased baking dish. Brush the chicken liberally with the glaze. Turn the pieces over, and brush again. Bake for 45 minutes, or until no longer pink. Make sure to remove the chicken halfway through and re-baste with the glaze.

Continued On Page 108

"A terrifying tale of
sluts and bolts."

frankenhooker's mango breast

frankenhooker

The fact that this movie kind of circles around the main character's fiancé dying in a tragic lawnmower accident really sets the tone of what you're in store for. *Frankenhooker* has a lot of the same elements to it as Re-Animator does; however, it is simply just not as good. Don't get me wrong though, *Frankenhooker* is special in its own way. It borders on being a slapstick comedy, but it still has a good amount of gore. Plus, there's even a pimp named Zorro. *Frankenhooker* is weird, funny, and worth every minute of film. Just make sure to grab yourself a mango-flavored breast first. Chicken breast people, geez, get your heads out of the gutter!

ingredients:

Frankenhooker's Mango Breast ingredients:
1 Mango, Peeled and diced
1/3 Cup Red Onion, diced
1/3 Cup Tomatoes, diced
¼ Cup Jalapeño, Seeded and diced
2 Tablespoons Cilantro
1 Tablespoon Lime Juice
1 Tablespoon Olive Oil
1 Teaspoon Minced Garlic
¼ Teaspoon Ginger
4 Chicken Breasts, boneless, skinless, and fat trimmed

Jeffrey Franken Fiesta Marinade ingredients:
1 Cup Silver Tequila
Juice from half a Lime
1 Tablespoon Hickory Liquid Smoke
1 Teaspoon Cumin

directions:

In a medium-sized bowl, mix together all marinade ingredients. Add the chicken, cover, and chill for 2 hours. Preheat the oven to 350 Degrees. Remove the chicken and transfer it to a small greased baking dish. Bake for 45 minutes, or until no longer pink.

In the meantime, heat up the olive oil in a medium-sized saucepan. Add the onion and jalapeño, and sauté for 5 minutes over medium-low heat. Next, add all the remaining ingredients, and sauté for 5 minutes, then cover and simmer for an additional 5 minutes on low heat. Serve the chicken with a generous amount of mango salsa over the top.

Serves 4

fried carrie chicken

carrie

The movie *Carrie* encompasses every reason why I never attended Prom, and showcases just how rude people can be. I have to admit, I kind of wish this movie was real life. If it were, then maybe people would stop being passive-aggressive bullies on the internet and have a fear that someone with telekinesis powers will make the roof cave in on them. Just nix the whole "catching on fire" part. Carrie 1, Student body 0.

ingredients:

Fried Carrie Chicken ingredients:
2 Pounds Chicken, pieces of your choice, bone in with skin
2 Cups All-purpose Flour
1 Teaspoon Seasoning Salt
1 Teaspoon Paprika
1 Teaspoon Black Pepper
1 Teaspoon Dry Mustard
Vegetable or Peanut oil for frying

Maniac Mommy Marinade ingredients:
3 Cups Buttermilk
½ Cup White onion, diced
¼ Cup Parsley, diced
1 Tablespoon Garlic Powder
1 Teaspoon Black pepper
1 Teaspoon Cayenne Pepper
½ Teaspoon Salt
½ Teaspoon Thyme

directions:

In a large baking dish, mix together all the marinade ingredients. Next, add the chicken, cover, and then chill for 24 hours.

The next day, in a large bowl, mix together all the chicken ingredients except the chicken and oil. Preheat the oven to 350 Degrees. Also, heat the oil in a large deep pan or a deep fryer to 350 Degrees. If using a pan, do not fill it more than ½ way up with oil. Create an assembly line, and take chicken out of the buttermilk mixture and dip it in the flour mixture to fully coat. Repeat this step by then dipping it back into the buttermilk and then coating in the flour mixture; this will make your chicken extra crispy. Fry the chicken in the oil until brown and crisp. Dark meat takes about 13 to 14 minutes, and white meat usually 8 to 10 minutes. After the meat is fried, transfer it to a baking dish, and bake in the oven for another 20 minutes or when you cut it open it is no longer pink on the inside.

Serves 4

HENRY

Retrato de un asesino

"The shocking true story
of Henry Lee Lucas."

henry: portrait of a pulled pork sandwich

henry: portrait of a serial killer

There is something about serial killers that I find fascinating. Even as a child, I was always intrigued by the darkness behind people. Nevertheless, I don't think my 8th grade teacher was too stoked when I chose this topic for class speech day. Meh, what are you going to do? *Henry: Portrait of a Serial Killer* is one of the most screwed-up movies I have ever seen. In real life, I don't believe Henry Lee Lucas ever lived in Chicago; however, most of this film is shot in the city, and particularly close to an area I used to live in. Can you say CREEPY?! Like a lot of serial killers, Henry loved killing women, had a thing for necrophilia, was a violent psychopath, and (I'm going to go out on a limb here) probably did all this stuff because he couldn't find a decent pulled pork sandwich. It may be too late now to turn back the hands of time, as Henry died in prison at the age of 64 due to heart failure, but I like to think I could have saved lives with this Dr. Pepper-infused and BBQ sauce-soaked pulled pork sandwich.

ingredients:

Henry: Portrait of a Pulled Pork Sandwich ingredients:
2 Pounds Pork Tenderloin
1 (18 oz) bottle Sweet Baby Rays Sweet and Spicy BBQ sauce
1 (2 Liter) Dr. Pepper
¼ Cup Light brown Sugar
1 Tablespoon Liquid Smoke
1 Teaspoon Cayenne Pepper
1 Teaspoon White Vinegar
Crockpot or Slow Cooker

Trashy O'Toole's Buttery Buns ingredients
6 Buns, circular and thicker cut
3 Tablespoons Butter, melted
Garlic Salt

directions:

Pour the Dr. Pepper into a slow cooker. Add the brown sugar, liquid smoke, cayenne pepper, and vinegar; mix to combine. Add the pork tenderloin and mix to completely coat. Use a big spoon to help pour the liquid mixture over the meat. Cover and cook on low for 7 hours. After 7 hours, drain the meat and pull it apart with a fork. Return the meat back to slow cooker and mix in the bottle of BBQ sauce. Cook for 1 more hour.

To make the buns, melt the butter and slightly brush the top and bottom of each bun with butter. Lightly sprinkle a small amount of garlic salt on each. Broil for 3-5 minutes, or until toasted. Serve the pulled pork in between each bun.

Serves 6

"To avoid fainting, keep repeating: "It's only a movie, only a movie, only a movie…"

the last lamb burger on the left

the last house on the left (1972)

The original *Last House on the Left* was all kinds of messed up, with a side of disturbing for good measure. The film was made in 1972 and was banned off and on in the UK until 2002 and in Australia until 2004. The film's distribution companies, Hallmark and Atlas International in Germany, attempted to release it as a snuff film. Don't for a second think that getting a US release was all handshakes and hugs either. When Wes Craven first took the film to the MPAA, they slammed it with an "X" rating. This didn't work for Mr. Craven, as he really wanted an "R" rating for a wider release. Ultimately, he cut 20 minutes out of this movie and was still denied an "R." As we've all learned over the years, sometimes it's about whom you know more than anything, and Craven found a friend on the film board. He then put all the cut scenes back in, and his friend pushed it through with an "R" rating. That's what I call Jenga, folks.

directions:

To make the Terrifying Convict Tzatziki sauce, dice up the cucumbers and place them in a bowl lined with a paper towel. Sprinkle with salt, and then fold the paper towel over the cucumbers and flip them upside down. This will allow the excess water to drain out of the cucumbers, as to not make your sauce to runny. Allow to sit for 1 hour. After, discard the paper towel and pour out any water. Return the cucumbers back to the bowl and add the garlic, mint, and lemon juice. Mix to combine. In a medium bowl, add the Greek yogurt and sour cream. Gently fold the cucumber mix into the yogurt mix until just incorporated. It's important to not over mix, as you will break down the yogurt too much, causing it to become overly liquid-ish. Add salt and pepper to your liking, and then cover and refrigerate for 2 hours.

In a large bowl, combine all the burger ingredients except the lamb; stir to combine. Add the lamb to the mixture and stir until well incorporated. Form the lamb into 6 burgers. In a large skillet, heat up the olive oil, and then cook the lamb patties for 6-8 minutes on each side, or until completely cooked.

To make the buns, mix the melted butter with the garlic and rosemary. Lightly brush the tops of each bun with a little of the butter mixture. Toast on broil for 3-5 minutes. Place one patty on each bun with a generous amount of tzatziki sauce.

Makes 5

ingredients:

The Last Lamb Burger on the Left ingredients:
1 Pound Ground Lamb
2 Pieces of Bread, torn into small pieces
1 Egg, Beaten
¼ Cup Parsley
2 Tablespoons Whole Milk
1/3 Cup Red Onion, diced
½ Cup Crumbled Feta
1 Teaspoon Minced Garlic
1 Teaspoon Marjoram
1 Teaspoon Rosemary
½ Teaspoon Oregano
½ Teaspoon Cumin
½ Teaspoon Salt
½ Teaspoon Black Pepper
2 Tablespoons Olive Oil, for frying

Terrifying Convict Tzatziki ingredients:
1 (8 oz) Greek Yogurt
2 Tablespoons Sour Cream
1 Tablespoon Fresh Mint, chopped
1 Tablespoon Minced Garlic
1 Cucumber, Diced
1 Teaspoon Lemon Juice
Salt and Pepper to Taste

Brutal Biting Buns ingredients:
5 English Muffins
1 Tablespoon Butter, melted
1 Teaspoon Garlic salt
½ Teaspoon Fresh Rosemary, Stems discarded and diced

*"Who will survive and
what will be left of them?"*

leatherface loaded burger

texas chainsaw massacre

Over the years, Leatherface has quickly grown to be a household name. This chainsaw-wielding maniac is the perfect amount of creepiness, terror, and unanswered questions. Not to mention he is a master with the meat hook. *The Texas Chainsaw Massacre* can be credited as one of the top movies to bring attention to the horror genre, and I for one am grateful. I'm also even more grateful that the 2003 remake didn't make me want to cry and put myself through therapy. Much like the tagline, these loaded burgers will not survive long on your plate, and nothing will be left of them.

ingredients:

Leatherface Loaded Burger ingredients:
1 ½ Pound Lean Ground Beef
2 Eggs
½ Cup Red Pepper, diced
¼ Cup Dry Breadcrumbs
3 Tablespoons Whole Milk
½ Cup Green Onions, diced
½ Cup Mild Cheddar, shredded
1 Tablespoon Garlic, minced
1 Teaspoon Black Pepper
1 Teaspoon Salt
4 English Muffins
1 Tablespoon Olive Oil

Road Trip Roasted Fennel ingredients:
1 Fennel, leaves cut and discarded, bulb part chopped
2 Tablespoons Olive Oil
1 Tablespoon Balsamic vinegar
1 Teaspoon Mined Garlic
Salt, Pepper, Red Pepper Flakes, and Brown Sugar to taste

The Spicy BBQ Chainsaw Massacre ingredients:
½ Cup Ketchup
¼ Cup Honey
2 Tablespoons Worcestershire Sauce
1 Tablespoon White Vinegar
1 Teaspoon Ground Mustard Seed
1 Teaspoon Brown Sugar
1 Teaspoon Onion Salt
1 Teaspoon Red Pepper flakes
½ Teaspoon Paprika
½ Teaspoon Cinnamon
¼ Teaspoon Salt

directions:

Preheat oven to 400 Degrees. Cut the bulb off of the fennel, chop it up, and then lay the pieces out in a baking dish. In a small bowl, mix together the oil, vinegar, and garlic. Pour this mixture over the fennel and toss to coat. Next, sprinkle with a little salt, pepper, red pepper flakes, and brown sugar. Bake, covered, for 25 minutes.

Heat the olive oil in a large skillet over high heat or while preheating the grill, if that's the way you prefer to cook your burgers. In a large bowl, mix together all the burger ingredients except the English muffins. Form the mixture into 4 patties, and cook for 5 minutes on each side or to your liking.

To make the BBQ sauce, combine all the ingredients in a small saucepan, and bring to a boil over medium heat. Once the boil happens, turn the heat down to low and simmer for 5 minutes, uncovered.

Crisp up the English muffins by placing them on a baking sheet and setting the oven to broil. Cook for 1-2 minutes. Next, assemble the burger by placing some roasted fennel on the bottom muffin, followed by the patty, and then a generous amount of BBQ sauce. Top off with the top of the English muffin.

Makes 4

maniac meatball sub

maniac (1980)

Why is it that so many men have "mommy issues?" Whether it's that they can't cut the umbilical cord or that they want you to wear their mother's face, this garbage is annoying! All you ladies out there, I'd put money on the fact that you've probably dated at least one mama's boy in your lifetime, and probably wanted to run for the hills. Hopefully for you though, it wasn't a mama's boy named Frank. If it were, you'd likely be missing your scalp at this point and a creepy mannequin would be the new owner. This sounds an awful lot like a Lifetime movie...shivers! So what do you say, let's start a movement to put all mamas' boys at bay, and what better way to do it than with a kryptonite only known as the Maniac Meatball sub. After all, it's the perfect combination of sweet and tangy, and when in a time crunch can be easily made with pre-packaged meatballs.

ingredients:

Maniac Meatball Sub ingredients:
1 (16 ounce) Package Meatballs
1 (28 ounce) Bottle Sweet Baby Ray's BBQ Sauce
1 (12 ounce) Jar of Apricot Preserves
1 Loaf of French bread, cut into 6 inch pieces or use precut sandwich buns

Caramelized Hooker Onions ingredients:
1 Sweet Onion, chopped
1 Tablespoon Olive Oil
1 Tablespoon Light Brown Sugar
1 Tablespoon Balsamic Vinegar
½ Teaspoon Cayenne Pepper

directions:

In a small saucepan, heat up the olive oil and cook the chopped onions on low heat for 15 minutes, stirring frequently. After 15 minutes, add the remainder of the ingredients and cook, covered, for another 15 minutes. In a medium-sized saucepan, bring the BBQ and preserves to a boil. Add the meatballs and cook for another 10 minutes on medium heat, stirring frequently. Assemble the sub by putting 2-3 meatballs into the cut bread followed by a generous amount of onions. Next, on a baking sheet, put the sandwich into the oven and bake with the broiler on high for about 5 minutes, until the bread becomes slightly crunchy.

Makes 4

HERBERT WEST
HAS A GOOD HEAD
ON HIS SHOULDERS...
AND ANOTHER ONE
ON HIS DESK.

H.P. Lovecraft's classic tale of horror

RE-ANIMATOR
...It will scare you to pieces.

"It will scare you to pieces."

re-animeatloaf

re-animator

When are people going to learn that bizarre experiments never end well? Sure, they make for great storylines, but the experiments usually mean that your ability to do basic things like keeping all your body parts in the right order or, oh say, staying alive tends to lack. I guess that is unless you're a virgin, then sometimes you get the "get out of death free" card. *Re-Animator* is one of my favorite movies. I think the fact that nobody that had hands in creating this movie took themselves too seriously is what ultimately won my heart. It is graphic and perverted, yet overly silly in nature and provides a brilliant, mad-scientist-esque performance from Jeffrey Combs as Herbert West. After all, what's more fun than the fact that there were 25 gallons of fake blood used in making this movie? So, when you're done gawking at all the fake blood, move onto this meatloaf that packs a lot of flavor into a small ball of fury. I can guarantee you one thing - this isn't your mama's meatloaf!

ingredients:

Re-Animeatloaf ingredients:
1 ½ Pounds Lean Ground Beef
1 Cup Onion, diced
½ Cup Green Pepper, diced
½ Cup Red Pepper, diced
¼ Cup Carrot, grated
2/3 Cup Milk
2 Slices of Bread, torn into pieces
2 Eggs
½ Cheddar Cheese, shredded, extra to garnish
½ Cup mozzarella, shredded
2 Celery Stalks, diced
¼ Cup Parsley, chopped
½ Cup Soy Sauce
1 Tablespoon Honey
1 Teaspoon Dijon Mustard
1 Teaspoon Worcestershire sauce
1 Teaspoon Liquid Smoke
½ Teaspoon Hot Chili sauce
½ Teaspoon Black Pepper
¼ Teaspoon Cayenne Pepper
1 Cupcake baking tray

Mad Scientist Sauce ingredients:
1 (8oz) Can Tomato Paste
1 Tablespoon Ketchup
1 Teaspoon Mustard
1/3 Cup Brown Sugar
1 Teaspoon Garlic Powder

H.P. Lovecraft's Mash ingredients:
3 ½ Pounds Russet Potatoes, peeled and diced
¼ Cup Milk
1/3 Cup Cream Cheese
1 Tablespoon Butter
1 Tablespoon Minced Garlic
4 Fresh Chives, diced
½ Teaspoon Salt
½ Teaspoon Black Pepper

directions:

Preheat oven to 350 Degrees. First, start with the Meatloaf: in a large bowl, beat the eggs. Add the milk and bread, and allow to sit for 5 minutes. Stir in the remaining ingredients and mix well. In a lightly greased cupcake tray, spoon the meatloaf mixture into each circle until completely filled and slightly over the brim. In a small bowl, mix together all the sauce ingredients, and then baste the tops of each cupcake meatloaf with some; save extra sauce for later. Bake for 50-60 minutes. Take it out of the oven once, halfway through cooking, and gently tip the tray over the sink to allow some of the grease to drain out. Baste again with a small amount of reserved sauce and return it back to the oven.

In the meantime, make the mashed potatoes. Take a large saucepan and fill it about 75 percent of the way full with water; bring to a boil over high heat. Add the potatoes and cook for about 20 minutes, or until potatoes are soft. Remove from heat and drain the water out of the pan. Next, return the potatoes back to the saucepan over low heat and add the cream cheese, butter, and garlic. Stir and mash to completely combine the ingredients until a typical mashed-potato consistency forms. Stir in the milk and chives. Taste and add more salt and pepper to your liking, then set aside.

Once the meatloaf is cooked, allow them to slightly cool, and then remove them from the cupcake tray. Pipe a generous amount of mashed potatoes over the top, as if you were frosting a cupcake. Sprinkle with a little extra cheese and serve.

Makes 12

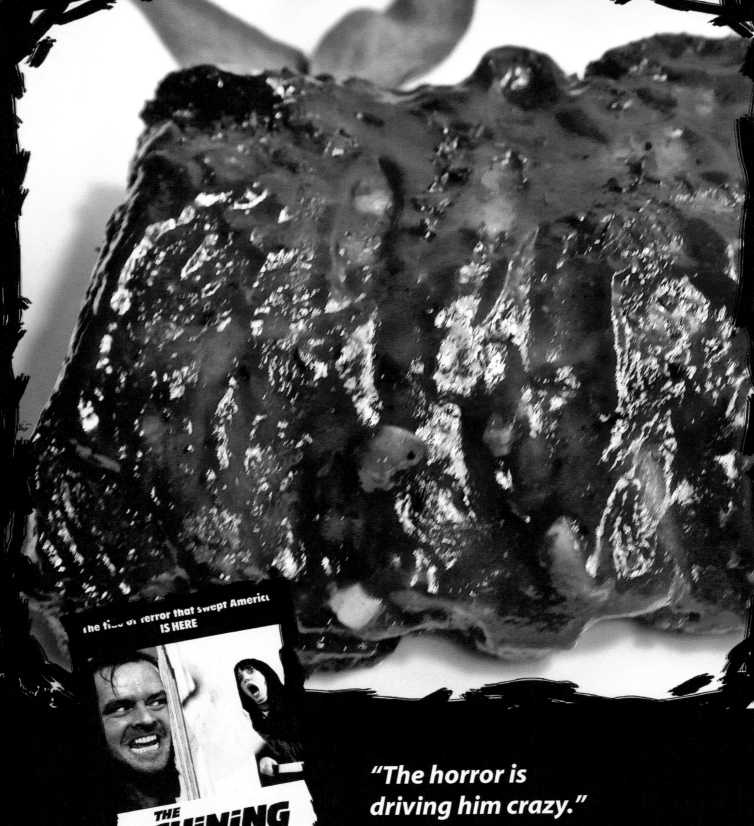

"The horror is driving him crazy."

redrum ribs

the shining

I would love nothing more than to spend one full day just hanging out with Jack Nicholson. One day, that's all I ask for. We can write stories, talk to the dead, play with axes, and drink whiskey. I'd probably pass out instantly from the fumes of the whiskey, but it would be awesome nonetheless. *The Shining* is on a lot of people's "Top 5" lists, and for a good reason. On some levels, the movie is untouchable. In the areas it may be lacking, Stephen King makes up for it with the TV mini-series of the same name, released in 1997. If you haven't gotten your hands on this yet, I suggest doing so, as it touches a bit more on the ghostly aspect of *The Shining* and follows the book a bit more literally. So, if I ever get that magical call from Jack Nicholson, I'll make sure to invite you all along with me; we can yell "Heere's Johnny," whip up some Redrum Ribs, and then slightly lose our minds together.

ingredients:

Redrum Ribs ingredients:
2 Slabs Pork ribs, about 1 pound each
1 (18 oz) Bottle of your favorite BBQ sauce
Nonstick Foil

Lunatic Liquid Rub ingredients:
1/3 Cup Mustard
¼ Cup Red Wine
2 Tablespoons Honey
1 Tablespoon Worcestershire Sauce
3 Garlic Cloves, crushed and diced

The Kubrick Rub ingredients:
½ Cup Brown Sugar
1 Tablespoon Onion Powder
1 Tablespoon Salt
1 Teaspoon Paprika
1 Teaspoon Thyme
1 Teaspoon Chili Powder

directions:

In a small bowl, mix together all the Lunatic Liquid rub ingredients. In another small bowl, mix together all The Kubrick Rub (dry rub) ingredients. Lay 1 slab of rib out on a large piece of foil, and fold the sides and ends up to form a pocket that won't allow the liquid to fall out. Repeat with the other slab. Spoon half of liquid rub over each slab of rib and spread around to evenly coat. Next, sprinkle half the amount of dry rub over each rib on both sides. Use your hands to liberally rub the mixture into the meat. Fold the foil tightly around each slab, making sure nothing can escape. Allow it to marinate in the refrigerator for 24 hours.

In a large Crock Pot or slow cooker, cook both slabs for 8 hours on low. After 8 hours, remove the ribs and transfer them to a baking dish. Lightly baste each slab bottom and top with your favorite BBQ sauce. Set the oven to broil, and cook for 5-10 minutes, or until a sticky-glazed look starts to happen. Make sure to watch when broiling though, as you do not want to burn the BBQ Sauce.

Serves 2-4

UN GATTO
NEL CERVELLO
[Nightmare Concert]

"You will slowly be
possessed by madness."

sloppy joe in the brain

cat in the brain

Cat in the Brain is in my top 5 favorite movies of all time. I don't care what anyone says, this movie is brilliant. I wouldn't expect anything less from a movie that had an original script of 49 pages and contained no dialogue, but only had descriptions of bodily mutilations and sound effects that would compliment them on-screen. Lucio Fulci successfully makes a movie were he plays himself going crazy, at a point in his life were he was rumored to have really been going crazy. So the question really is: are we watching a movie or a documentary? If you think you're a gore connoisseur, then I dare you to amp it up a notch, and watch some *Cat in the Brain*-style limb amputation while devouring this tasty, modern day sloppy joe.

ingredients:

Sloppy Joe In The Brain ingredients:
1 ½ Pounds Ground Beef
½ Onion, diced
½ Cup Poblano Pepper, diced
3 Garlic, diced
1 (6 ounce) Can Tomato Paste
½ Cup Water
2 Tablespoons Ketchup
2 Tablespoons Brown Sugar
1 Tablespoon A1 Sauce
1 Tablespoon Red Wine Vinegar
1 Tablespoon Chili Powder
1 Teaspoon Dried Oregano
½ Teaspoon Mustard
½ Teaspoon Salt
¼ Teaspoon Nutmeg
¼ Teaspoon Black Pepper
Salt to taste

Texas Toasted Limb Buns ingredients:
Loaf of French Bread, cut into 1-inch pieces
½ Cup Butter
1 ½ Teaspoons Minced Garlic
1 ¼ Teaspoons Garlic Salt
½ Teaspoon Parsley
1 Teaspoon Chives
Foil

directions:

Preheat oven to 400 Degrees and slice the loaf of bread horizontally but without cutting all the way through - you want the slices still attached at the base. In a small bowl, mix together all the Texas Toasted Limb Buns ingredients except for the bread. Next, spread a little bit of the butter mixture onto each side of the cut bread and press the loaf back together. Wrap the loaf tightly in foil and bake for 15 minutes.

In a large skillet over medium-high heat, sauté the ground beef for 5 minutes. Add the onion, garlic, and poblano pepper, and sauté for 5 more minutes, or until the onions are tender. Drain the fat out. Next, mix in the tomato paste and water; stir until the paste is diluted down. Mix in all the remaining ingredients. Continue to cook over medium-low heat, stirring occasionally for 5 to 10 minutes, or until the mixture is thick. Serve sloppy joe mix in between two pieces of Texas toast.

Makes 6

"Unequivocally the most terrifying movie I've ever seen." —AFTER DARK Magazine

EVERY BABYSITTER'S NIGHTMARE BECOMES REAL...

WHEN A STRANGER CALLS

COLUMBIA PICTURES in association with MELVIN SIMON PRODUCTIONS presents
A BARRY KROST PRODUCTION
CHARLES DURNING   CAROL KANE   COLLEEN DEWHURST
WHEN A STRANGER CALLS
Also Starring TONY BECKLEY
RACHEL ROBERTS   RON O'NEAL   Executive Producers MELVIN SIMON AND BARRY KROST
Music by DANA KAPROFF   Written by STEVE FEKE   Directed and FRED WALTON
Produced by DOUG CHAPIN and STEVE FEKE

"...Fear is the message."

when a stuffed date calls

when a stranger calls (1979)

The first 20 minutes or so of this film is killer…no pun intended. The suspense and the concept, bravo Mr. Fred Walton, for you single handedly crushed young girls hopes and dreams of babysitter stardom everywhere. The idea of some maniac's creepy prank calls coming from none other than the house you are sitting in… well, I know I was never the same afterwards. In 2006, *When A Stranger Calls* got an unfortunate reboot that was lacking much of the flavor the first possessed. Bacon-wrapped dates have been all the rage lately, and in the trending of reboots, this is my reboot of the classic recipe. However, I promise you all my reboot won't fall flat on your taste buds, and there's a good chance you'll probably want to drink half of this spicy and sweet red pepper sauce as you are making it.

ingredients:

When A Stuffed Date Calls ingredients:
16 Slice of Bacon
16 Dates, Cut vertically and pitted
½ Pound Spanish chorizo
Toothpicks

Sweet And Stalker Red Pepper Sauce ingredients:
14 oz Can Diced Tomatoes
15 oz Jar Roasted Red Peppers
1 Small Tomato, chopped
½ White Onion, chopped
3 Garlic Cloves, crushed and diced
½ Jalapeño, Seeded and chopped
½ Cup Red Wine
¼ Cup Water
1 Tablespoon Oregano
1 Teaspoon Sugar
½ Teaspoon Basil
½ Teaspoon Red Pepper flakes
1 Tablespoon Dark Chocolate
½ Teaspoon Salt
¼ Teaspoon Black Pepper
1 Bay Leaf

directions:

In a small saucepan over high heat, bring the canned tomatoes, red peppers, water, red wine, and chopped tomato to a boil. Turn the heat down to low, add the remaining ingredients, and cook covered for 2 hours, stirring occasionally. Remove the bay leaf, and with an immersion blender or in a blender, puree all the ingredients until smooth. Return back to saucepan, and add additional salt and pepper to your liking.

Preheat oven to 350 Degrees. To assemble the dates, make a vertical slice in each, but be careful to not slice all the way through the date; you want to almost create a pocket. Discard the pit, and then fill comfortably with the chorizo. Wrap each stuffed date with a piece of bacon and secure with a toothpick.

In a medium-sized baking dish, heap 2 large spoonfuls of sauce into the dish and spread around the bottom. Next, put the bacon dates in the baking dish and drop about 1 tablespoon of sauce on each. Bake for 40 minutes. If you want the bacon extra crispy, turn the stove to broil and cook for 2-5 more minutes. Serve the dates in a shallow bowl filled partially with red pepper sauce.

Serves 3-4

FIRST THEY GREET YOU,
THEN THEY EAT YOU.

BLOOD
DINER

"First they greet you,
then they eat you."

blood diner milkshakes

blood diner

Blood Diner is as ridiculous as it is good. What's not to love? There's an entire nude aerobics class that gets gunned down, a zombie feast at a rock concert, and a guy who gets his hands cut off but still manages to open his door, start his car, and turn on his windshield wipers. *Blood Diner* is a wonderful splatter comedy that pays homage to the infamous Herschell Gordon Lewis film Blood Feast. It features two young men who do the bidding of what's left of their crazy uncle sitting in a jar. Mike and George Tutman run a lovely cafe with a little twist: they serve the leftover body parts of "unclean women," unbeknownst to their dining guests. Where do the rest of the parts go, you ask? Well, they all get stitched together to help resurrect a cannibalistic goddess, of course!

This milkshake may or may not be tastier than unclean women, but it contains three of the best things ever: nutella, peanut butter, and cookie dough ice cream. Oh and don't worry, no virgins were hurt in the making.

ingredients:

2 Cups Chocolate Chip Cookie Dough Ice Cream
½ Cup Whole Milk
¼ Cup Nutella
2 Tablespoons Peanut Butter
Reese's® Peanut Butter Cups, crushed to garnish
Fudge, melted to garnish
Sea Salt, to garnish

directions:

In a blender, mix together the ice cream, milk, nutella, and peanut butter. Put melted fudge in a piping bottle and make swirls along the inside walls of a medium-sized glass. Don't worry if it doesn't look perfect or the chocolate runs a little, that's what it makes it better!

Next, pour the milk shake mixture into each glass. Top off with a little crushed peanut butter cups and a pinch of sea salt.

Makes 1

*"Alive…without a body…
fed by an unspeakable
horror from hell!"*

the brownie that wouldn't die

the brain that wouldn't die

So there is this man, and he is stricken with the love bug for a woman who ends up decapitated. Of course he proceeds to do what any normal man would in this situation: keep the brain and build a new body around it. Yes, I'm sure that plot line sounds familiar, but having been released in 1962, *The Brain That Wouldn't Die* was one of the first to use it. As a matter of fact, the movie itself was actually filmed in 1959, but due to various legal and censorship problems, it couldn't be released until years later. Yes, it's low budget, it's grimy, and it even has a title goof at the end referring to itself as The Head That Wouldn't Die, but I wouldn't change this film for the world. Well, maybe I would for these soft, chewy brownies.

ingredients:

1 Cup Butter, melted
2 Cups White Sugar
4 Eggs
2 Teaspoons Vanilla Extract
¾ Cup Unsweetened Cocoa Powder
¼ Teaspoon Salt
1 Cup Flour
½ Teaspoon Baking Powder
¼ Cup Sour Cream
10 Oreos®, I used the holiday addition for the red color
½ Cup White Chocolate chips, ¼ cup more to garnish
¼ Teaspoon Chili Powder

directions:

Preheat oven to 350 Degrees. Lightly grease a 9x13 Inch baking pan. Melt the butter and pour it into a medium-sized mixing bowl. Stir in the sugar and vanilla, and mix until just incorporated (for about 1 minute). Next, add the eggs one at a time, beating after each addition. Next, add the cocoa powder and beat until well-blended. Follow by adding the sour cream and mixing again until well-blended.

In a separate bowl, combine the flour, baking powder, chili powder, and salt. Slowly add the flour mixture to the batter, mixing constantly. Next, fold 6 crushed Oreos® and white chocolate chips into the batter. Pour the batter into the pan, top with 4 more crushed Oreos® and ¼ cup white chocolate chips, and then bake for 30-35 minutes. Let cool, cut, and then serve.

Makes 18

B-Rated Desserts

killbot balls

chopping mall

Not only does this film have a great name, I feel like within the next 10 years we aren't to far off from it happening. That is, if the Rapture doesn't decide to kick in beforehand. *Chopping Mall* is all the typical '80s cheese you can want, packed into a little bundle with killer robots. An unfortunate group of teenagers that work at the mall get together late one night for a party in one of the stores. Little do they know that, earlier in the day, a freak lightening accident occurred, turning the security robots into body-count-hungry killers. Through the night, the newly formed "killbots" attempt to off the teenagers one by one. If anything, this film has taught me that anything can become a weapon. In the same vein of *Chopping Mall,* this recipe has taught me that bacon goes good in anything. These donut holes consist of a maple-flavored batter which pairs perfectly with bacon. They are then brought to a whole new level with bacon's secret soul mate, chocolate and a pinch of sea salt. I'm drooling.

ingredients:

2 Tablespoons Apple Cider Vinegar
6 Pieces of Bacon, cooked and crumbled
6 Tablespoons Milk
1 Egg
2 Tablespoons Margarine
1/3 Cup White Sugar
¼ Cup Light Brown Sugar
1/3 Cup Maple Syrup
2 ½ Cups All-Purpose Flour
2 Tablespoons Instant Vanilla Pudding
2 Teaspoons Vanilla Extract
½ Teaspoon Baking Soda
½ Teaspoon Cinnamon
½ Teaspoon Pumpkin Pie Seasoning
¼ Teaspoon Salt
¼ Cup Milk Chocolate chips
1 Quart Oil for deep frying
Sea salt

directions:

Cook the bacon in a medium-sized skillet until slightly crunchy. Drain, crumble, and set aside. In a small bowl, mix together the vinegar and milk. Allow to sit for 10 minutes. In a large bowl, cream together the margarine and both sugars until smooth (about 1 minute). Next, add the egg, maple syrup, bacon, and vanilla extract. Mix until well-blended.

In a medium-sized bowl, sift together the flour, baking soda, salt, cinnamon, and pumpkin pie seasoning. Add half of the flour to the batter, followed by the vinegar mixture, and then the rest of the flour. Stir until fully blended. Fold the chocolate chips into the dough, and allow the dough to rest for 10 minutes.

Heat 2 inches of oil in a large, deep skillet to 350 degrees. Make sure your hands are covered in flour before you handle the dough, otherwise it will be difficult to form. Roll the dough into small donut holes and fry until golden brown, turning once. Make sure to make small holes, because if you make them to big they will have a hard time cooking evenly through the center. Drain on a paper towel, sprinkle with the sea salt, and allow to completely cool (about 20 minutes).

Makes 20

"I'm so proud of my boys. They never forget their Momma."

mother's day cake batter cakes

mother's day

Mother's Day is '80s exploitation horror at its finest. It borders the same politically incorrect line as *Last House on the Left* and *I Spit on Your Grave*. In this case though, I actually think that, due to the rawness of the storyline, it makes the other two movies look like Pixar films. *Mother's Day* is about two sons who will do anything to impress their good ol' Ma. Murder, torment, nothing is too much when it's meant to please Mommy. Unfortunately, three unsuspecting woman found this all out the hard way. Are you disturbed yet? No, well then let's proceed in the form of the yummiest concoction on earth, cake batter cupcakes. These little muffins of fury make the idea of licking the mixer beaters not only acceptable, but encouraged. They're firm like a cupcake plus gooey with batter in the center, and they are topped off with a colorful palette to wow the eyes. Dare I say this is perfection, even to a maniac Mommy's standards? Yes…I think I do.

ingredients:

Mother's Day Cake Batter Cakes ingredients:
1 (8oz) Cream cheese, softened to room temperature
3 Cups All-Purpose Flour
3 Eggs
1 ½ Teaspoons Baking Powder
¼ Teaspoon Salt
1 ½ Sticks Unsalted Butter, softened to room temperature
1 Cup Buttermilk
1 ½ Cups Sugar
1 ½ Teaspoons Vanilla Extract
½ Cup White Chocolate chips
¼ Cup Sprinkles, extra to garnish

Rose F(ROSS)ting ingredients:
1 (8oz) Cream cheese, softened to room temperature
½ Stick unsalted butter, softened to room temperature
1 ½ Cups Powdered Sugar
2 Teaspoons Vanilla Extract
Food Coloring of your choice

directions:

Preheat oven to 350 Degrees. Line a muffin tin with cupcake liners. Sift together the flour, baking powder, and salt, and set aside. In a large bowl with a mixer on high speed, cream together the butter, cream cheese, and sugar until smooth (about 3 minutes). Add the eggs one at a time, mixing gently after each addition. Next, add half of the flour mixture, followed by the butter cream, followed by the remaining flour. After each addition, mix until just incorporated. Fold in the vanilla, sprinkles, and white chocolate chips. Do not over-mix.

Pour the batter into the lined cupcake tin, filling each area 3/4th of the way full. Reserve the leftover batter for later. Bake for 15 minutes. You want the outside of the cupcake to be firm enough to be sturdy, but you want the center to still be slightly gooey, so be careful to not over-bake. Allow the cupcakes to cool, and then with a sharp knife, cut out a slight shallow circle on the top of the cupcake in the center. Fill each hole with 1 Teaspoon of the leftover batter and then put the cut-out top back in the hole.

To make the Rose F(Ross)ting, beat together the cream cheese, butter, and vanilla extract. Add the powdered sugar to the mixture ½ cup at a time, mixing after each addition until incorporated. Next, add as many drops of a food coloring of your choice to the frosting to tint to your liking. Remember the rule of thumb, though: gel food coloring tends to work a little better than liquid food coloring. If to much liquid food coloring is added, it can make your frosting become slightly watery and/or unstable. Whenever I can, I stick with gels, and I have become a huge fan of the Wilton line if you're curious. Pipe on the frosting, and then top off with a little bit of sprinkles.

Makes 16

ORGY OF THE DEAD

Come...Let Me Take You In My GOLDEN ARMS..!

IN GORGEOUS and SHOCKING
ASTRAVISION SEXICOLOR

with CRISWELL and
A BEVY of BEAUTIFUL GIRLS!

FOR ADULTS ONLY!

Produced by ASTRA PRODUCTIONS
SCA DISTRIBUTORS

*"A Masterpiece of
Erotic Horror!"*

orgy of the beer battered cupcakes

orgy of the dead

I don't think it would be right to do a section on B-Movies and not include *Orgy of the Dead*. After all, this film is listed in the top 100 Most Amusingly Bad Movies Ever Made in the book "The Official Razzie Movie Guide." If that isn't an accomplishment, then I don't know what is. In order to get John's creative juices flowing, he and his girlfriend Shirley head out to find a cemetery. Little do they know that they will soon crash their car and be forced into a graveyard filled with the dancing dead under the glow of a full moon. There's lots of nudity, tons of dancing, and just the right amount of weirdness that I couldn't even begin to explain it all to you in one paragraph. The moral of the story: watch this movie. At least if you hate it, you can play a sweet drinking game with these booze cupcakes by taking a bite every time a stripper's boob bounces.

ingredients:

Orgy of the Beer Battered Cupcake ingredients:
1 Cup Imperial Mokah, reserve 2 tablespoons for the frosting
2 ½ Cups All-purpose Flour
½ Cup Buttermilk
½ Cup Vegetable Oil
¾ Cup Unsweetened Cocoa Powder
3 Eggs
¼ Cup Sour Cream
1 ½ Cups Sugar
½ Cup Brown Sugar
1 Tablespoon Baileys Irish Cream
1 Tablespoon Vanilla Extract
1 ½ Teaspoons Baking Soda
½ Teaspoon Pumpkin Pie spice
½ Teaspoon Chili Powder
¼ Teaspoon Salt

Prisoner Peanut Butter Frosting Ingredients:
3 Cups Cream Peanut Butter, make sure to use a good brand
4 Cups Powdered Sugar
2 Sticks Unsalted Butter, at room temperature
2 Tablespoons Imperial Mokah
2 Teaspoons Bailey's Irish Cream
Milk chocolate, grated

directions:

Preheat oven to 350 Degrees and line a muffin tin with paper liners. In a medium-sized bowl, whisk together the cocoa, sugars, flour, pumpkin pie spice, salt, chili powder, and baking soda, then set aside. Pour the beer into a large glass and allow it to settle for 5 minutes before using. In a large bowl, combine the beer, buttermilk, Irish cream, vegetable oil and vanilla. Add the eggs one at a time, mixing after each addition until fully incorporated. Gradually mix the dry ingredients into the wet ingredients, and mix until just combined. Next, add the sour cream and beat until thoroughly combined and smooth.

Pour the batter into the lined cupcake tin, filling each area 3/4th of the way full. Bake for 20-25 minutes, or until a toothpick inserted into the center comes out clean. Frost with the Prisoner Peanut Butter Frosting.

In a large bowl, cream together the peanut butter and butter until light and fluffy. Add 1 cup of the powdered sugar, and beat until combined. Next, add the beer and Irish cream to the frosting; lightly mix until just incorporated. Add the remainder of powdered sugar and thoroughly mix. If you want the frosting slightly thinner, add a little milk. If you want it thicker, add more powdered sugar. Pipe onto the chocolate beer cupcakes, and then garnish with grated milk chocolate.

Makes 18

"He's the death of the party!"

scarecrow gone whoopie pie

scarecrow gone wild

Is there such a thing as an "F" rated movie? If not, can we make one solely for this movie? *Scarecrow Gone Wild* features another wrestler turned actor, Ken Shamrock. Only this time it's not as smooth of a transition as in *They Live*. On the other hand, *Scarecrow Gone Wild* has something *They Live* doesn't - a homicidal scarecrow. I haven't decided if this is a good or bad thing yet, though. The few things I have learned from this film, however, are the following: scarecrows can whistle underwater; daylight can come, disappear again, and then return all within a 5 minute sequence; and when someone is attempting a punch, even if they miss by a good two feet, said victim will still fall over. If these aren't some life-changing lessons, then I don't know what are.

Life-changing lessons also come in the form of two miniature cakes known as the Whoopie Pie. Today's life lesson is that you can take childhood favorites and make them into semi-adult desserts. Ladies and Gentlemen, I give you a S'mores Whoopie Pie.

ingredients:

Scarecrow Gone Whoopie Pie ingredients:
1 Stick Unsalted Butter, at room temperature
1 Cup Superfine Sugar
¼ Cup Light Brown Sugar
½ Cup Buttermilk
2 Cups All-purpose Flour
1 Teaspoon Baking Soda
1 Teaspoon Salt
1 Teaspoon Vanilla
½ Cup Unsweetened Cocoa Powder
2 Eggs

Spring Break Crème Filling ingredients:
1 Stick Unsalted Butter, at room temperature
1 (7 ounce) Jar Marshmallow Crème
1 Cup Powdered Sugar
1 Teaspoon Almond Extract
1 Teaspoon Honey

Ken Shamrock Chocolate Graham Cracker Drizzle ingredients:
3 Ounces Hershey® Milk Chocolate Baking Chocolate
Graham crackers, crushed to garnish

directions:

Preheat oven to 350 Degrees. Lightly grease 2 large cookie sheets. In a medium-sized bowl, mix together the flour, baking soda, salt, and cocoa powder, then set aside. In a large bowl with a mixer on medium speed, cream together the butter, brown sugar, and superfine sugar. Beat until the mixture becomes pale and fluffy (about 5 minutes).

Next, add the eggs one at a time, beating after each addition until combined. Follow by adding half the flour mixture, then the buttermilk, and then the remainder of flour; make sure to mix well after each addition. Add the vanilla and mix until just combined.

Spoon the dough in 2 Tablespoon mounds onto the greased cookie sheets. Make sure to space them about 2 inches apart to leave room for rising. Bake for 11-15 minutes, or until the cakes are puffed and an inserted toothpick comes out clean. Transfer with a spatula to a cooling rack, and proceed to making the filling and frosting.

In a large bowl with an electric mixer on medium speed, beat all ingredients for the Spring Break Creme Filling until smooth (about 5 minutes).

For the Graham Cracker Drizzle, in a medium-sized and heat-proof bowl, melt the chocolate in the microwave. Transfer the melted chocolate to a piping bottle. Assemble the Whoopie Pies by spreading a generous Tablespoon of the Spring Break Crème Filling onto half of the cooled chocolate cakes - make sure to spread it on the flat side. Put the other cake halves on top of the spreaded fillings to form sandwiches. Drizzle the melted chocolate liberally over the top of each assembled sandwich, and then sprinkle them with a generous amount of crushed graham crackers. Serve warm.

Makes 6

continued directions:

Continued From Page 71

Farmhouse Gravy ingredients: In a medium sauce-pan bring 2 cups of chicken broth to a boil over medium heat. Add onion and pepper and continue to cook covered for 10 minutes. In the meantime, heat up milk in a small saucepan over medium heat. Discard onions, and add bouillon granules stirring until they have dissolved. In a medium sized bowl mix together flour and ½ cup chicken stock. Next, gradually stir flour mixture into saucepan, followed by heated milk. Stir to combine. Bring the mixture to a boil and cook stir-ring constantly until it has thickened. Stir in browning liquid until you have the color you like.

Survival Stuffing ingredients: Preheat oven to 350 Degrees F. In a large saucepan over medium heat, melt butter. Next, add all ingredients except, bread cubes, eggs, and chicken stock. Sauté mixture for 10 minutes, and then turn off the heat. Stir in chicken stock, and mix to combine. Add the bread cubes 1 cup at a time, gently stirring to coat after each addition. In a small bowl whisk both eggs together and then fold into the bread mixture until fully incorporated. In a large sized baking dish, bake stuffing covered for 30 minutes. Remove foil, stir, and continue to bake for 5 minutes longer or until slightly toasted on top.

Night of the Thanksliving Day Pizza: Preheat oven to 425 Degrees F. Roll out biscuit dough into a circle on a pizza tray leaving it about 1 inch thick. In a medium bowl, mix 2 ½ cups of stuffing with 1 cup of gravy. Spread the stuffing mixture on top of the biscuit crust. Follow with a layer of the turkey. Finish with 1 Cup of Mashed potatoes. Top with a generous amount of fresh chives and a sprinkle of black pepper. Bake for 10-15 minutes, or until crust is a golden brown.

Serves 4-6

Continue From Page 75

Begin cooking the rice in a large saucepan of boil-ing water for 10-12 minutes, or until tender. Drain out the water, and then allow the rice to com-pletely cool. Once cooled, heat the oil and add the minced garlic. Sauté for 1 minute, and then add the cooked rice, chili powder, rosemary, saffron, and parsley; sauté it all together for another minute. Push the rice to the side of the pan, and then pour in the beaten eggs. Mix together until the eggs begin to form a scrambled egg texture. Add the soy sauce, and mix well. Serve the chicken breast chopped up over a bed of rice.

Serves 4 as small portions or 2 as large portions

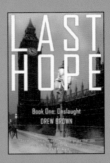